WHAT'S YOUR NEXT?

WHAT'S YOUR
NEXT?

THE BLUEPRINT FOR CREATING YOUR FREEDOM LIFESTYLE

DR. DAVID PHELPS, DDS

Published by Advantage, Charleston, South Carolina.
Member of Advantage Media Group.

ADVANTAGE is a registered trademark, and the Advantage colophon is a trademark of Advantage Media Group, Inc.

Printed in the United States of America.

10 9 8 7 6 5 4 3 2

ISBN: 978-1-64225-190-6
LCCN: 2020914711

Cover design by David Taylor.
Layout design by Megan Elger.

This publication is designed to provide accurate and authoritative information in regard to the subject matter covered. It is sold with the understanding that the publisher is not engaged in rendering legal, accounting, or other professional services. If legal advice or other expert assistance is required, the services of a competent professional person should be sought.

TreeNeutral

Advantage Media Group is proud to be a part of the Tree Neutral® program. Tree Neutral offsets the number of trees consumed in the production and printing of this book by taking proactive steps such as planting trees in direct proportion to the number of trees used to print books. To learn more about Tree Neutral, please visit **www.treeneutral.com**.

Advantage Media Group is a publisher of business, self-improvement, and professional development books and online learning. We help entrepreneurs, business leaders, and professionals share their Stories, Passion, and Knowledge to help others Learn & Grow. Do you have a manuscript or book idea that you would like us to consider for publishing? Please visit **advantagefamily.com** or call **1.866.775.1696**.

To my three dads—my biological father, Herschel R. Phelps Jr.;
my real estate dad, Jack Miller; and my business and marketing dad,
Dan Kennedy—each of whom inspired me along the way to my "next."
To my much better half, Kandace, who loves me for who I am and who
allows me to continue my path to purpose, meaning, and significance
in life. And to my daughter, Jenna, who, through her health challenges,
has taught me more about myself, perseverance,
and what life is really all about.

Grab your free bonus gift
from Dr. David Phelps now
at FindYourNext.com/Gift.

CONTENTS

FOREWORD

Dan Kennedy

I've had the pleasure of working with David Phelps as a private client and Titanium Mastermind member for a number of years. His tenacity and perseverance in transitioning from his active income career as a dental professional to the founder and CEO of Freedom Founders is a testament to his credibility in authoring *What's Your Next*.

David extols new rules of the road. In a world where everyone desires freedom, options, and security, but not everyone takes risks to achieve them (or has the resolve to maintain them), this book presents a formula for those ready to embark on a different path.

David embodies all the characteristics of one who does not follow the majority but who lives life and does business on his own terms and is not dictated to by others. He is a renegade. Throughout his life, he has created his own alternative path to work and wealth, where wealth can be used to work for him and not just him for it. In these pages, he shares how readers can buck the traditional path and follow him toward financial and personal freedom.

As David has experienced, there's more payoff in self-improvement than any other type of improvement, and for this reason, he encourages others to invest in themselves. He also understands the benefits of surrounding himself with winners and investing in his relationships. He has always sought the best in mentors and coaches and participates in multiple Mastermind Groups each year. Jim Rohn aptly states, "You become the average of the five people with whom you most associate." David has constantly upped his average.

Too many people are servants to their businesses. I have long insisted that a business must serve the owner. David exemplifies this mantra. He has intentionally designed his business passion to revolve around his life, his family, and his freedom. He chooses who he works with, when and how he works with them, and where he works with them (all of David's clients go to him, not the reverse, something I have promoted nearly all my life).

David wisely resists commoditization and has created unique differentiators into his business, beginning with *who he is* and with much less emphasis on *what he does*. This is a wealth multiplier that most will never achieve; instead, most focus on the limiting technical aspects of the "doing of the thing" (e.g., doctor, dentist, lawyer, butcher, baker). Commoditization is the prelude to extinction.

David spent his entire career questioning the traditional approach to work and wealth. Never one to buy into the constructs of the status quo, he discovered the most powerful question you can ask: *What's your next?* Through his own discovery process and life story, David dispels the myths and misinformation that have been handed down generation to generation, leaving those who would follow the majority to live lives of quiet desperation.

The biggest single difference between successful people and the mediocre majority is how easily they take no for an answer. While he had to deal with many naysayers, David never accepted the limiting beliefs of others and charted his own course to ultimate freedom. This behavior has more to do with success than anything else.

His path to success was not a straight line. He had to deal with multiple adversities in his pursuit of freedom, beginning with multiple health crises of his daughter, a failed marriage, and an unsuccessful business sale. Napoleon Hill stated, "Every adversity, every failure, every heartbreak, carries with it the seed of an equal or greater benefit." David turned his adversities into opportunities for change, never stopping to cry foul or claim that life is unfair.

David portrays five levels of freedom, the first being financial freedom. From there, one has the ability to choose by intention how he uses his time; the relationships in which he wishes to engage; the prioritization of personal health; and ultimately, the real purpose, meaning, and significance in one's life.

He started pursuing financial freedom in earnest while a first-year student in dental school, being the only student in a class of 140 to invest in a rental property. Four years later, David split $50,000 in capital gain profit with his father, his joint venture partner, and went on to leverage it into multiple investment properties, which was the basis of his financial freedom (replacing his active income with passive income) by age forty-one.

This book will dispel many of the common traps of societal rules for success, like our state-run education system and the false pursuit of an elusive retirement goal. If you are an entrepreneur in spirit who is frustrated by the traditional career path of work, sacrifice, and wealth building and who craves an alternative path to work smarter and generate wealth and income that works for you, this book is for you. David will show you how to reinvent yourself and your means of making money and how your business and money can be structured to work for you.

Wake-Up Call

On August 25, 2004, the surgical floor of Texas Children's Hospital in Houston is humming with activity as medical personnel dart from one room to the next, treating kids, providing comfort, and saving lives. A gurney is parked in front of the surgical suite doors and is encircled by staff—doctors, nurses, anesthesiologists, phlebotomists—hastily prepping a young patient for surgery. One man stands apart from the medical team—a man in his forties, hunched and still amid the chaos. He barely notices the IV lines and EKG wires attached to the patient. He is focused only on the small hand wrapped in his, the big brown eyes more moist than usual, the bottom lip that quivers imperceptibly.

■ ■ ■

My daughter, Jenna, was diagnosed with high-risk acute lymphocytic leukemia at age two. After undergoing multiple rounds of chemotherapy over two and a half years, she began having epileptic seizures. In 2004, when she was twelve years old, she had a severe episode that left her vomiting blood on the floor. After her mother rushed her to the local hospital, she was airlifted to Dallas. Three days later she was diagnosed with end-stage liver failure. My daughter's spirit was strong, but her liver was not.

Jenna was placed on an organ transplant list, and the waiting began. In the meantime, her mother and I researched the best surgical hospital for when we got the call, and we ultimately decided on Texas Children's Hospital in Houston. Waiting was challenging, but since I had a busy dental practice at the time, I tried to distract myself with work and patients.

One Wednesday, as I was consulting with a patient, my front desk staff member tapped me on the shoulder. My first response was irritation; I didn't like to be bothered when I was with a patient, but I quickly realized the interruption was warranted. My staff told me I had an urgent phone call. Immediately, I had a lump in my throat because I knew it had to be about Jenna, and when there was news about her, it was rarely good.

I grabbed the phone and heard a kind voice say, "Dr. Phelps, I've got good news for you." It was the transplant nurse coordinator, and she announced they had a liver for my daughter. She explained that time was critically important. Things would move rapidly. In fact, Jenna and her mother, who had prepared their bags months before in preparation for this call, had already left for the hospital. Her mother and I had hoped for so long that Jenna would be in good enough health to receive a liver if and when we were ever so fortunate to get the call. Here we were. It was go time.

The clock was ticking. Every second mattered. My heart was pounding, and I was sweating as I told my staff the news and raced out the door. They had all been prepared in case this day might come, and they knew what to do in my absence. I headed straight to the airport and flew to Houston. When I arrived at the hospital, staff quickly ushered me to the surgical ward on the third floor.

I got there just in time to see my daughter splayed on a gurney, with medical personnel bustling around her. I had never felt so helpless. I realized that all of my education and training to become a dentist—all of the wisdom, experience, and money I'd accrued along the way—didn't mean a damn thing.

Nothing else mattered but this—holding her hand for one more moment before they wheeled her away from me. Out of my arms. Out of my sight. Out of my control. All I could do was pray.

When they pushed her through the operating door, I was frozen in place. I was her father, but I couldn't protect her, I couldn't heal her, I couldn't take her place—I couldn't do anything but love her and pray.

I did a lot of thinking in the following hours as I awaited news of my daughter's condition. I wondered about some of the decisions I had made in my life. How many choices had I made unconsciously? How many times had I followed a path simply because those before me had trodden the same trail? How could I reclaim control of my life and my choices? How could I make my family's lives better? How could I live my life without regrets?

Six hours later, the surgeon come out and reported that the operation was complete and deemed a success. I realized I had been holding my breath for hours, days, weeks, maybe years. I could finally breathe. My child was okay. Jenna was transferred to the intensive care unit to begin her long journey toward recovery. It would be challenging, but I knew she had the tenacity and the courage to fight as she always had.

Though her liver transplant and early health issues feel far behind us in many ways, they forever changed our lives. After that day in the hospital, feeling worthless and desperate for more time, I never viewed my career, finances, or personal goals in the same way.

That day was my wake-up call: I made the decision to alter my life and my daughter's life on my own terms. I would no longer make choices unconsciously or unintentionally. I stared at my daughter's face, resting in the ICU, and promised her, *No more.*

As a young adult, I laid out my entire life in advance. I was blessed with good intellect and a strong work ethic. Failure was never an option. I *would* have a perfect family. A perfect life. A perfect professional dental career. My journey, however, was not linear. It was a zig, a zag, one step forward, two steps back. It wasn't perfect, as I had planned; in fact, it was often disrupted and left me seeking more.

Over the years, as my family dealt with one health crisis after another, all that was once stable and constant started to crumble. My marriage with Jenna's mother ended, and I started seeing more and more cracks in the perfect life I aspired to build. I started questioning how my time was spent. As Jenna's health continued to deteriorate, I tried desperately to remain in control. If I was successful and a good provider, then maybe I could help navigate the increasingly dire journey my family was embarking on.

I wanted security for my family, and I had worked hard for it. Yet all the things I had done in my life—all the hard work I put in, all the training, the school, the education—still didn't give me what I wanted. What did I want? I always assumed I sought wealth like my peers. More money was not going to save my daughter, though; more money was not going to buy more time with her. Then it was clear: what I wanted more than anything was *time*.

Though I had always been a planner, Jenna's illness reminded me there was no backup plan for running out of time. Jenna's needs snapped me out of thinking everything had to be long term. In the past, I always planned down the road. I thought that as soon as I completed my various to-do lists, *then* I would be fully engaged with my life. I called this "someday syndrome," and it was an insidious trap in which I fell prey.

It was when standing alone outside the operating room, feeling helplessly out of control, that I questioned this traditional mindset. Am I doing the right thing? Am I still living my life the way I should? Do I get another chance? Does my child get another chance?

I had to make a decision: Was I going to build a life that afforded me the freedom of time with my daughter, or would I take the traditional path and give away my time to the career and business I'd spent decades building? It was a moment of truth. My life—and my daughter's—depended on it. There were no more excuses.

> I had to make a decision: Was I going to build a life that afforded me the freedom of time with my daughter, or would I take the traditional path and give away my time to the career and business I'd spent decades building?

WHAT'S AHEAD?

Traditionally, young people choose a path and stick to it through schooling and their early adult years. I know I was driven and focused quite early, so when I chose the medical field, I never wavered. I have no regrets about my dentistry career. It brought me a great deal of satisfaction and certainly served me well for over twenty years, but in my heart, I was always an entrepreneur.

If I had been offered a glimpse of a viable alternative career path through entrepreneurship, I may have achieved freedom decades earlier. All I knew, however, was that an antitraditional career seemed risky. I thought having a profession was the soundest long-term investment. I have since learned that these ingrained, fear-based beliefs limited me and thwarted my journey toward personal and financial freedom.

I have spent the last thirty years blazing a trail from the traditional path of work and wealth building to an alternative one that leads to true freedom—doing what you want, when you want, with whom you want, where you want.

Over the last ten years, I have built a platform called Freedom Founders™ that has allowed me to focus on coaching families and speaking to audiences, as I live out my purpose to help as many people as possible be Free for Life™, no longer trading time for dollars. Since its inception in 2010, Freedom Founders has blossomed from a group of twelve into a tightly knit community that has helped hundreds of professional practice owners and small business owners achieve peace of mind through reliable and secure real estate investments that make retirement not just a goal but a reality.

Our Free for Life members have completed their Freedom Blueprints™ (customized road maps engineered to create predictable and sustainable annuity cash flow from highly curated real estate investments) and have reached full freedom in life and can live fully with all options of "What's next?" before them.

Through the following pages, I offer these same proven Freedom Founders strategies to anyone who desires to create wealth and achieve a deeper level of freedom. This book is for anyone who has an entrepreneurial spirit and is frustrated by the traditional career path of work, sacrifice, and wealth building. It's for anyone who craves an alternative path that allows them to work smarter and generate wealth and income that *works for them*.

Some readers may have already taken steps down the traditional path, and that is okay. Certainly with the price of education and training, it's difficult and costly to reverse course. Even so, I will provide a blueprint to start building wealth today that will ultimately afford the freedom of choice tomorrow.

Using my own story as an example, readers will gain proven strategies to convert transactional income—what you make from career, business, or job when you trade time for dollars—into assets that will start producing wealth and recurring annuity cash flow by themselves, thus offering you the financial permission to consider alternative paths that suit you and your family's needs.

Throughout the book, I will introduce some of my clients and colleagues, many of whom chose a traditional path they never doubted until they were in their fifties and sixties and nearing their retirement age. At that point, they began questioning "What's my next?"

Some of that questioning was financially motivated as they wondered how they would continue to enjoy full lives on limited incomes. Others debated how many more years they would work before their golden years could begin. Even those who were more financially free still questioned how they might spend their time and energy once they attained personal freedom. Despite the reasons behind the questioning, the answer remains the same: to find freedom, you must determine "What's your next?"

Like my Freedom Blueprint Workshops, this book offers a detour from the traditional path and shows that life is not a single track from formal education into a profession; it's not a one-way course with no exits. Setbacks happen—divorce, illness, business failures. Too often we see successful people and assume their paths were easy. As I will share from my own life and the lives of my clients, this is rarely the case. More often, successful people have found ways to turn adversity and challenges into opportunities.

As I learned that day standing outside the operating room as my daughter fought for her life, wake-up calls can hit you hard and fast. Not if, but when, setbacks happen, they are occasions to question your paths and patterns. Oftentimes wake-up calls have the potential to afford you greater prospects than you could have imagined.

Wake-up calls can shift your entire reality. Pursuits can change, and priorities can reshuffle in an instant. That day in the hospital, I had an epiphany about what I really wanted to pursue. It wasn't money; it was freedom of time and resources. I wasn't sure how I would get there, but it was instantly imperative that I figure it out.

> Wake-up calls can shift your entire reality. Pursuits can change, and priorities can reshuffle in an instant.

What I have learned since my wake-up call is that money will indeed buy time if I'm intentional about it. Up to that point, however, I was on a hamster wheel, doing what society said I needed to do: work hard. Jenna's liver transplant suddenly gave me a reason to step back, reconsider my priorities, and make deliberate, bold changes to transform my family's lives. Ultimately, after twenty-one years in business, I would sell my successful dental practice. Why would I take such decisive actions? Jenna was my *why*. Next I needed to answer "What's my next?"

I'm happy to report that Jenna did recover from her liver transplant. Now, at age twenty-seven, she is a published author, speaker, and student training for a career in physical therapy. I've relished watching her evolve into a tenacious young woman with an indomitable spirit.

More than a decade ago, I made the daring choice to detour from my traditional career path in pursuit of something more. Was it easy? No. But my subsequent time spent with my daughter, watching her find her path and chart her course, has been my greatest reward.

As I will share in the following chapters, after my wake-up call, I used my active income as a young dentist and practice owner to invest in real estate. By the time I was forty-five, I had enough capital invested to step away from my practice full time to spend more time with my family.

Making that decision altered everything in my life. Today, I continue to use that capital to generate annuity income, allowing me to focus on coaching families and speaking to Freedom Founders audiences, as I live out my purpose to help as many people as possible stop trading time for dollars.

Throughout these pages, you will discover a guide to "What's your next?" using my freedom-based approach to work and wealth. Using my own experiences and those of my clients and colleagues, you will discover how you can boldly invest your time, energy, and finances into a freer future for yourself and your family.

To live an unconventional life, you have to do unconventional things. You can't just follow the majority and hope. If you want to reach freedom sooner, the truth is that you must take as active a role in your finances as you did in your career. It's a choice, and the sooner you decide "What's your next?" the sooner you will discover your own path to freedom.

CHAPTER 1

What's Your Next?

Chris: "I built a successful dental practice with my wife, Julia, in Greensboro, North Carolina. It was hard work and demanded everything I had. For so long my mind was cluttered with stress, problems, and worry. I had little time to read, listen, and absorb the world outside of dentistry.

"I built a respectable investment portfolio on Wall Street and in commercial real estate. The traditional model seemed to be working. I was nearing retirement, and I was excited. But in 2007, the market turned, and I lost almost a third of our investment principal overnight. I thought I would be stuck behind the dental chair into my seventies. My hopes of retirement were crushed."

Julia: "Those early years were tough. Chris and I had a small dental practice and put in a lot of hours. With me having my dental background, I could run the front desk and be the dental hygienist. I loved it.

"After the financial crisis, we did not see an end to our professional stress, and probably Chris more so than me. He was always passionate about his career and patients, and he loved dentistry. Toward the end, however, there was none of that.

"When you see someone that you love and care about going through such anguish, it is difficult. Those days were probably the hardest days I've ever had with Chris. We just didn't see an end to our crisis.

"He was always driven to find a new source of income, but freedom is even more than that: freedom is peace of mind. Chris was the one who found Freedom Founders. He wanted to give it a try, and I'm so glad we did."

Chris: "Today, I've sold my practice, but my retirement paychecks exceed what I used to make as a dentist. Now I am financially free. I read what I want and listen to speakers I'm interested in. I have time to think. I golf. I travel. I spend more time with my family.

"I now have a passion and a desire to make an impact on people's lives by helping them become financially and personally free. I want to impart the ability to live each day to its fullest, on one's own terms, without the concern or worry of financial constraints. That feeling is so liberating, and that's why passing that on to others has become my purpose."

■ ■ ■

When I first met Chris and Julia, I immediately recognized their combined compatibility and work ethic. As a couple who had shared backgrounds in dentistry, they worked hard to build a family practice they were proud of. When the financial crisis hit, they lost much of their financial assets in the stock market. Their hard-earned aspirations about being able to leave the practice were crushed. They didn't see an end in sight, and retirement was suddenly a luxury they might never experience.

Being a resourceful and capable pair, they tried various ways to create multiple income streams outside of dentistry, including Amway, nutritional supplements, and other multilevel marketing schemes. Those options did not work out. When they received an email from Freedom Founders, Chris was willing to try one more option. He had to convince Julia, but they did end up joining us in Dallas for a conference.

I remember at the first session Chris sat near an exit door with his arms folded across his chest and a skeptical look on his face. This was a posture I had seen before. I knew he wanted and needed something to work, but he'd been through so many other pathways that didn't lead him where he wanted to go.

After the conference, they decided to join Freedom Founders Elite Mastermind Group—a community of like-minded professional practice owners (primarily dentists) who were within three to five years of desired exit or transition out of active practice. As Chris and Julia soon learned, while Freedom Founders' unique ability is in highly curated real estate investment strategies, our mission is freedom and generational legacy. Members often refer to Freedom Founders as "my tribe" or "my people." It is a place where they feel safe and understood, no longer feeling obligated to project success but instead to openly discuss life, business, and finances.

During the three years that Chris and Julia worked through the program, I coached them on my proven process called the Freedom Blueprint, a customized road map engineered to create predictable and sustainable annuity cash flow from highly curated alternative (real estate) investments. Over time, they began to redeploy their assets into real estate, which provided them definitive and sustainable cash flow, and they were eventually able to sell their practice and find the freedom they had sought for years.

Once Chris and Julia achieved freedom and retired out of their active income, they understood the power of asking, "What's my next?" They decided they wanted to continue the Freedom Founders legacy and assist other professionals in discovering an alternative path toward financial and personal freedom.

Since that time, Chris has become a leader in our group and onboards our new members. Considering that he has been in the same position that many of our new clients find themselves in, he is perfectly suited to prepare them for the transformative process of asking, "What's my next?"

Chris and Julia's story is quite common. Many of my clients come to me after trying the traditional path of work and wealth— some of whom have spent decades there. Despite their varied careers and professions, all clients are united by their search for an alternative approach.

They are all wondering, "What's my next?" My role is to mentor people as they answer this question for themselves, and in the process, collaborate with them on how to make their wealth work for them. As Chris and Julia experienced, the Freedom Blueprint allows people to stop sacrificing and pursue what's most important in life: relationships, purpose, legacy, and freedom.

ARE YOU STUCK ON A TRADITIONAL PATH?

Anyone with an entrepreneurial spirit who is interested in an alternative path should be asking "What's my next?" As Chris and Julia suspected, there was a better way to approach work and wealth than trading time for dollars—one that prioritized freedom. Like many people, they were stuck on the traditional path of wealth building.

ARE YOU STUCK ON A TRADITIONAL PATH OF WEALTH BUILDING?

- Are you maxing out your debt with school loans, credit cards, and an entitlement lifestyle?
- Are you stuck in a traditional financial "accumulation model" hoping to have enough to last you through your retirement years?
- Are you sacrificing your entire working life, trading time for dollars, until you're in your sunset years?
- Are you locking up your hard-earned dollars in a retirement 401(k) or IRA, waiting until you're sixty when the dollars are finally available to you?
- Are you planning to live on an ever-dwindling fixed income in retirement, hoping that it'll be enough to last?
- And are you working so hard for your wealth, when instead you could make your wealth work for you?

From my experience with clients and colleagues, asking "What's my next?" redefines how you approach life. Without an understanding of the question or the answer, there is only vertical movement, with no room for lateral growth. When you don't question your trajectory, you may find yourself on a path that you didn't choose. You feel trapped, isolated, stagnant.

In my experience, the more successful a person is by society's standards, the more imperative it is to question your "next" because success often breeds complacency. You want to always have a desire for improvement—not just in your career choices but in all areas of life. You must be critically honest with yourself about your life and whether the career you've chosen is truly serving you rather than you serving it.

When you are on a traditional path, you are often bound by the trappings of work, debt, and sacrifice. You might be stuck in a career rut, growing increasingly inadaptive or chasing a moving finish line.

On a traditional path, you often have the same profession for several decades. Since innovation propels our culture at a frenetic pace, people who choose one career and stick with it often feel isolated and opt to stay within their own industries, in their own networks, in their own bubbles. When this happens, growth and evolution are stunted. This is a dangerous mental space to occupy and is why many people lose their identities when they retire and no longer have their occupational motivation.

The traditional path of wealth building holds traps that can snare anyone, from teenagers considering college to veteran professionals considering retirement. As we will discuss throughout the book, these traditional paths aren't inherently bad. When you don't know there are alternate options, however, then you assume you have no choice.

What could be your opportunities instead become your trappings. This creates a vastly different mentality that is counterproductive to the freedom mindset. Freedom means choosing your life, from when you work, to where you vacation, to how and when you invest money.

Common traps of the traditional path include the following:

- Defining oneself by industry and societal norms

- Falling prey to the debt mentality

- Adhering to limiting beliefs and mindsets

- Following the traditional career plan

- Following the traditional financial investment plan

- Trading time for dollars

- Viewing retirement as the finish line

One of the first traps of the traditional path is being defined by industry and societal norms. Many of my clients and colleagues have lived long, industrious careers before retiring and finding that their health and happiness have suffered. Why is this? Because their identities and worth were so tied in their occupations that they lost their vitality.

After years of training, practice, and sacrifice, too many people merge their personal identities with their professional roles. This sometimes leads to chasing the proverbial carrot. Suddenly you might find yourself needing to live like a dentist, doctor, or lawyer. You rate your success on whether you can appropriately meet those standards.

To break free from this trap, you must recognize that the ideal you hold is merely a mental construct. As you work to retrain your dependence on traditional pathways as the only options, you start to separate these societal expectations from personal realities.

Social media's burgeoning role in our culture only exacerbates our misplaced identities. Too often we become driven to cultivate the persona of our trade: we need to vacation to the destinations of a doctor; we need to live in the house of a doctor; we need to send our kids to the schools of a doctor. This hijacks our identity and can lead to pursuing more luxuries, more possessions, and frankly, more debt.

Debt has become so normalized in our society that it is slowly becoming an accepted by-product of maturation. If you go to college, for example, it's normal to graduate with debt. Furthermore, if you pursue a higher degree, it's common to start your career saddled with hundreds of thousands of dollars of debt. You may think, *I already have $250,000 in student loans; what's the harm in adding more?*

Unfortunately people enter willingly into this trap at a young age and are never fully freed from it. I work with many dentists late in life who still function under the trappings of exorbitant debt. If you are burdened by debt, no matter your active income, you will not feel the benefits of true freedom.

Another trap is living life with limiting beliefs and mindsets. These are often subconscious products of our environments—created by well-meaning parents, teachers, mentors, and community leaders. These are beliefs that are passed from one generation to the next with little examination. For example, because your parent may have gone to college, then to graduate school, then to a career for forty years, you may chart the same course for yourself without question.

Limiting beliefs hold you back from what's possible. Gaining some distance allows you to objectively discern whether such beliefs serve you. If they don't, you can change course and take back your freedom. How can one gain some distance? The best answer would be to go to your "five," or your inner circle—we'll talk more about this in chapter 5—a mastermind or other informal board of advisers to help provide some objectivity to see your blind spots. It's impossible to provide that kind of input for ourselves, and we'll all need some objectivity at some point.

Another trap we rarely question is that of the traditional career and its specialization, which inherently boxes us in and ultimately contributes to a stunted mind and spirit. The ability to adapt is important. My generation went into careers assuming they'd spend the next thirty or forty years there. The feeling of graduating school after years of education, ready to take the first step on your chosen path, is exhilarating. Sometimes, however, it doesn't take long before that elation wears off and reality sets in.

A lot of my dental colleagues went to school with an idea of what dentistry would be like that was based on a decades-old model. Now many medical professionals who thought they would have their own businesses are graduating school with too much debt. The entire health industry continues to go through significant disruption. There is no status quo, if there ever was.

Change is occurring at light speed today, and degrees that once seemed very relevant are quickly becoming less so; therefore, adaptability and flexibility are key. Furthermore, it's too costly to run an individual practice today because the capital costs are too extreme and insurance companies are reducing reimbursement rates. There's a consolidation and a marginalization of that old model that many people planned their futures on. This is precisely why you need to be adaptive to the changing industry models.

A common mistake that ensnares people is following the traditional financial investment plan that calls for people to work hard, serve patients, save money, turn the wealth over to a financial adviser or Wall Street, and hope for the best. Sound risky? It is. But it's easy.

Nevertheless, it's what our parents did; it's what our grandparents did. In fact, because some people never question it or pursue alternatives, they assume this is the default financial investment plan. No one would consciously choose to lose money or squander earnings, but when you make unconscious, uninformed decisions, that's essentially what you're doing.

My clients often tell me their financial planners explained that they wouldn't need as much money when they retire because their major expenses—like their children and educational tuition—would be over. I call this traditional path a "shrinking to retirement" because it traps people into working longer and then retiring to a downsized life. Was that ever your vision of the future?

The goal is to transition out of or leave active income production from a job or career when one is still vital and healthy. After decades building careers and growing families, people actually want to do *more* than they used to. They want to travel and live fully, not assume a demure lifestyle and hope they have enough money to last the rest of their lives.

Another insidious trap is so common that it is rarely challenged: the trap of trading time for dollars. This mindset can be particularly damaging to one's mental and emotional health. Too many people trade their time—the most precious commodity—for dollars, and it rarely makes them more financially free. Advanced degrees and high specialization can provide a relatively high dollar-per-hour trade, but that in itself is a con—do you need to put yourself through the stress and financial burden of pursuing an advanced degree that really isn't essential for your practice?

> Too many people trade their time—the most precious commodity—for dollars, and it rarely makes them more financially free.

Recognizing this trap changed my mindset and my life. When I realized this trap was keeping me from having time with my child,

I was motivated to enact change. In selling my dental practice, I was able to break free, and my life was transformed.

As Chris and Julia learned through their own experience, one of the most detrimental traps is viewing retirement as a finish line. This is dangerous because if there is a finite end, then you limit yourself to a single track that you cannot deviate from. How many people spend their days in jobs they hate because they have only five more years, seven more years, ten more years until retirement?

When we realize that time is the greatest asset, then we start to understand why and how this mindset endangers us emotionally and psychically. Why do people dread Mondays and the start of a new week? Because they are not enjoying their lives spent doing things they'd rather not do, in places they'd rather not be, with people they'd rather not be with. That's the retirement construct. You do something that has become mundane—or worse, something you hate—for several decades and then exit to what? The question should never be "What's my end?" because that is fixed and static. Asking "What's my next?" instead inherently positions you to grow, evolve, and excel.

Chris and Julia were typical of hardworking professionals who considered retirement their endgame. Like many, they glorified retirement as a demarcation between their current life and their ideal life: *when I retire, I will take up fly fishing; when I retire, I'm going to learn Italian; when I retire, I am going to spend time with my family.*

There are several problems with this mindset, the first being that retirement is a goal line that keeps moving. Because of decreasing income, higher taxation, increased cost of living, and rising health costs, that finish line perpetually moves farther away. Oftentimes when a person does make it to retirement, they crawl across the finish line, financially and emotionally spent, only to realize that the dream they'd held firmly to for decades is in reality years of a diminished lifestyle.

In my Freedom Blueprint Workshops, I often use the metaphor of climbing a mountain to describe an idealized retirement. When you're at the base, you look up, see the mountaintop, and identify that as your goal: retirement.

In reality, however, retirement is climbing the mountain with switchbacks and meandering paths and arriving at the summit only to find you are not climbing one mountain but rather a series of crags. What you thought were the hard parts were actually only the beginning of a long, arduous journey that you may not have been prepared for mentally, emotionally, or financially.

Too often retirement is viewed as climbing a single mountain, when in reality, it is often scaling a series of summits and the valleys in between.

Retirement is a leftover term from the industrial age that is no longer relevant in today's culture. Because of medical technology and rising consciousness about health and nutrition, people are staying active and vital well beyond the traditional retirement age.

As long as someone is functioning well mentally and physically, why should they "complete" their work? They can remain vital members of the working sect and should be. In fact, some might argue that in the second half of life, after receiving training and decades of work and life experiences, a person is more adept at contributing to their communities, industries, and professions than ever before. For this reason, instead of using the term *retirement*, I prefer the word *evolvement*.

The entire concept of retirement is a trap. It creates a pattern of working for the sake of money—not for the mental, emotional, and spiritual benefits. You trade time for dollars, and you race toward a finish line that perpetually eludes you.

When I first met Chris and Julia, they had scaled their mountain only to discover there was rough terrain ahead with no finish line in sight. Their spirits were low from the journey, made worse because they had no guide. For them, retirement was like a mirage they saw in the distance that faded each time they rounded a corner. This can be so damaging to a person's spirit, vitality, and purpose.

When I work with clients who have fallen prey to these traps, I help guide them to a freedom point. This doesn't mean they quit anything; it just marks a passage into "What's their next?" They gain realistic expectations of what's ahead and excitement about the opportunities that exist.

With my customized Freedom Blueprint plans, there is no retirement, just evolvement. You're moving freely to "what's next." You're changing. You're fully engaged in your life. That's the ultimate freedom.

HOW CAN I DISCOVER WHAT'S MY NEXT?

Asking yourself "What's my next?" allows you to plan an exit from the traditional path and start using work and wealth to become Free for Life. Outside the financial and personal freedoms associated with this question, there is an emotional component as well. For this reason, there always needs to be a next.

As long as your mind and body are functioning well, there are always productive endeavors that can validate your worth and purpose.

> As long as your mind and body are functioning well, there are always productive endeavors that can validate your worth and purpose.

It's not going to happen magically, however. It needs to be an intentional endeavor. If there's not even the potential for something next, then there won't be.

Finding your answer to "What's my next?" positions you to make decisions based on your own interests, needs, and wants. Changing the way you think is the first step toward freedom. It can give you direction and an exit plan—not an exit to nothing but an entrance into a new path that leads to freedom.

Discovering "What's next?" is less about where you start and all about where you go. Wherever you are today is fine, but don't fall into the trap of staying in that place for too long. This breeds stagnancy, complacency, and boredom. Always be looking and asking how you can continue to keep an open mind, build additional skill sets, and explore new passions and curiosities.

FOLLOW-UP QUESTIONS THAT HELP ANSWER "WHAT'S MY NEXT?" INCLUDE THE FOLLOWING:

- How can I continue to evolve into a better and more valuable person, not only to myself but to the people I serve? My family? Whatever client base or customer base I enjoy? How can I continue to evolve and not stay stuck?

- Where am I today? What have I invested in to get to

where I am today in my career, business, or job?

- What gives me energy, and what takes it away?

Many people may not ask, "What's my next?" until they are in their fifties, sixties, or seventies at the end of their careers. Maybe they are financially safe but are seeking something rewarding outside their specified profession. Maybe they are pursuing ways to remain significant and relevant in their space if they haven't already found another passion outside of their careers. Without asking, "What's my next?" you can become diminutive in your thinking. Maybe your answer is less about your financial viability and more about your spiritual viability.

Others, like Chris, Julia, and myself, asked, "What's my next?" because of external circumstances. Chris and Julia were tossed about by financial upheaval outside their control. Their next was more about financial freedom than personal evolution at the time. That does not mean, however, that their next didn't provide them with both rewards.

In my own life, it was Jenna's liver transplant that woke me up and dared me to deviate from the norm. Although Jenna's health issues were challenging, I am thankful that I was cognizant to question my next but even more thankful that I was bold enough to pursue the answer.

For me, it has been incredibly rewarding to take my story, use it as a teaching tool for others, and build a business out of it. Most people my age are thinking about retiring or quitting, yet I have a new chapter of my life that lets me take what I once did and combine it with new skill sets and networks to enact change in myself, my family, and my community.

The question I am asked more than any other is, "David, why

aren't you retired?" What they mean is, "If you did so well with real estate and dentistry, why are you still going at it?" It's a fair question. It's true that I don't *need* to do anything.

For me, I do what I do because it's the most significant way I can invest my time. I have a genuine passion for helping my colleagues break the chains that enslave them to their professional practices. I want to help them overcome their financial fears, so they can create freedom in their lives and the lives of their families. This passion demands my attention. My world today is about impact.

Having the freedom to retire, and actually doing it, are worlds apart for me. I'll likely never retire in the typical sense. Remaining significant and relevant until my body and mind give out is my next.

Using my own life as a guide, my Freedom Founders approach to work and wealth provides more freedom, demands less sacrifice, and helps prioritize relationships, purpose, and legacy. I want to share how others might embark on the same journey and reap the same reward—freedom for life.

TAKEAWAYS:

- Determine in what ways you are trapped by the traditional path to wealth building.
- Don't follow the majority or live by others' agendas.
- Avoid falling prey to the debt mentality.
- Never question, "What's my end?" because that is fixed and static. Asking, "What's my next?" instead positions you to grow, evolve, and excel.
- Break free from limiting beliefs and mindsets that trap you into following the traditional career and financial models.

CHAPTER 2

Your Guide to Your Next

I am glad I am part of Freedom Founders. I expected I would be there listening about dentist stuff that probably wouldn't apply much to me, I would raise some capital, and that would be the extent of it. It has been so much more. What I have learned so far (in only three meetings) has changed the way I think about how to become free, financially independent, and live in a world of abundance.

—Greg Hughes

Since being in Freedom Founders, our lives have changed. I feel like we have clarity of purpose in our investing. Beyond that, we've found a group of like-minded individuals with whom we can network and grow. This group has really provided a home for us.

—Dr. Ben Jensen

Freedom Founders is a facilitator; it brings people together.

Freedom Founders is going to give you the tools to create your own action plan. Nobody is going to live your life for you, but if they can show you how it could be lived better, that's all you can ask for.

—Dr. Merril Rowe

■ ■ ■

My freedom-based approach to work and wealth is based on my own experiences finding an alternate path to financial and personal freedom. Though I ultimately discovered a different route to freedom, my own journey started on the traditional track I shared with my family and peers.

After high school graduation, I turned my attention to college. When I graduated from college, I immediately enrolled in dental school. My goal was the same one held by my dental peers—graduate and begin my career. After all, what would people say if I ditched the dental school degree for entrepreneurship?

My mindset wasn't there yet, so I caved—just like so many others. We didn't know any better. We didn't realize that there were viable options for our future outside the traditional pathway of higher education. Entrepreneurship? In the eighties, that was a euphemism for people with many dreams but no goals. No one with any ambition dare pursue a life without several degrees.

After graduation from dental school, I got married. Since my first wife was career oriented like myself, we opted not to have children right away. (In fact, it would be another nine years before Jenna was born.) Soon after our marriage, I started practice as an associate dentist with an established dentist. This scenario spared me from the burden of starting up a practice and figuring out all the things I didn't know about operating a business.

Once I began practicing dentistry, I found myself trapped in the traditional model of work. I spent long days at the office, away from my family. I rarely questioned this scenario—I saw it everywhere I looked. All of my friends from dental school logged equally long hours at the office and were thankful for the slivers of time they had with their families. Wasn't that enough for me also?

It wasn't until a few years into my dental career that I started questioning my path. Was I planning to continue this life for several more decades until retirement? Could I mentally and emotionally sustain dentistry for that long? Was there something more that I could offer? These questions continued to haunt me over the next twenty years of dentistry, even after I opened my own dental practice.

It wasn't until I had a child and watched her health struggles that I asked the right question, "What's my next?" More importantly than having the question in mind was finally having a reason to answer it *now*: Jenna. I knew I needed time with her, and I would boldly make that happen. It wasn't easy, but over the course of several years, I was eventually able to sell my practice—all thanks to the passive income I had been making doing rental estate investment on the side.

(Now's a great time to step aside and talk about the word *passive*. Passive income is a bit of a misnomer, implying there's no work involved in its maintenance. In reality, there is an active or semiactive effort required to take some control and orchestrate one's own financial future, though it's not the same as active or transactional income. Passive—or annuity or recurring—income is often created by putting the bulk of the time and effort in up front one time; finding the right people to invest through, as we provide in Freedom Founders; and performing due diligence, as we teach in Freedom Founders; and from there, yes, the income is relatively passive and needs only light management thereafter.)

After I sold my dental practice, I felt free, unmoored. Though I didn't know what my next step would be, it was exciting to step off the hamster wheel. I was able to spend time with Jenna and be there when she was sick. I got married to my current wife, Kandace, and we traveled and enjoyed our lives. I let go of the constant pressure I'd grown so accustomed to that I barely noticed. It was only in its absence that I realized how insidious and damaging it had been.

The Christmas after I sold my dental practice, Kandace decided we should send out a Christmas letter. With Jenna's health issues and surgery, life had been chaotic, but now with her recovery underway, Kandace thought it would be a nice time to update friends and family on the new changes occurring. Kandace drafted the letter, which explained that Jenna was doing well and that I had sold my practice.

Many of my friends in dentistry reached out over the following months asking, "I know *why* you left dentistry, but *how* did you do it?" Most of my colleagues were unaware that I had been doing dentistry by day and real estate investment by night and weekend for years.

I received numerous requests from other professionals to show them how I had left the traditional path. I told them I was happy to share with them, but if they were serious, why not piggyback on some of my investments? I figured this would be a good way to earn as they learned. I did this with several colleagues, and they soon shared their success stories within their own social circles.

By this point, I had been investing in real estate for twenty-five years and had built a strong network. I knew people who could find properties, people who could renovate them, and people who could manage them. I had learned how to negotiate and orchestrate good deals that solved problems for others and provided a solid investment opportunity for me. I began to see that my next could be linking medical professionals with real estate professionals. By connecting these two disparate networks, I could help people exit the traditional path and enter an alternate path toward financial and personal freedom.

In 2010, I invited these two groups to come together in what I called a mastermind meeting. With sixteen people in attendance, I described how the needs of one group might benefit the needs of the other. I was the translator between the real estate doers (deal creators or sponsors) and the potential investors (dentists and other professionals). I offered to lead this network for six months to see what might happen. After that, I explained that participants could choose whether to remain involved.

Six months later, every person reported that they wanted to continue the group. I was excited by their enthusiasm because I was having fun. I realized I loved connecting people and using my own journey to teach and assist others.

Ten years later, the Freedom Founders Mastermind Group currently has more than seventy members, including nine Free for Life members who have reached full freedom in life using my strategies and their customized Freedom Blueprint. Though the Mastermind Group was an organic evolution over the course of a decade, it quickly became my next and unlocked a new era of my life that has been dynamic, exhilarating, and truly rewarding.

Now I am free, having fun, living my purpose, and investing in my legacy. Though I began my own journey on the traditional path, it was when I asked myself, "What's my next?" that my life transformed.

MASLOW'S HIERARCHY AND THE FIVE FREEDOMS

When I meet new clients, the specifics of their pursuits are different, but the end goal is always the same: a good life. Quality of life is a difficult metric to track. You can't measure it with money—in fact, those who try often end up being the most miserable of all.

Abraham Harold Maslow was a legendary American psychologist in the early 1900s who spent decades attempting to discover how one might achieve this elusive quality of life. He created a framework for examining life critically and assessing the basic needs of humanity, which is now called Maslow's Hierarchy of Needs.

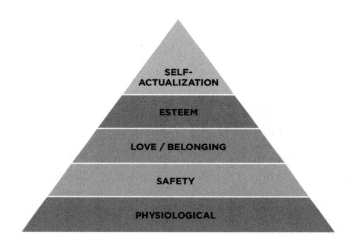

Maslow's Hierarchy of Needs depicts the basic needs of humans.

The Hierarchy of Needs is a useful starting point to understand what it means to live well. The hierarchy is a pyramid with five layers of needs. At the base are physiological needs—the need for food and drink, warmth and shelter, clothing, air, and sex. Once we're independent of our family of origin and we're out in the world, then we have to survive, and these are the fundamental building blocks of the human experience. When you're struggling with these basic necessities, it can feel like this is what life is all about. But in reality, this base of the pyramid is just the beginning.

When you have your basic physiological needs met, the next layer is safety, security, and freedom from fear. That might mean living in a better neighborhood; escaping toxic environments; or finding safe, secure relationships. When this need has been met, you feel like you can breathe easier. You have a small margin and aren't living paycheck to paycheck, for example.

The third level of Maslow's pyramid is about love and belonging. This layer is about finding your tribe—those people who think and feel the same way you do. Surrounding yourself with friends, family, and people who get you allows you to freely trust and love and be vulnerable. Meeting these needs means all the base needs are met. You're fed and comfortable, feel safe and secure, and have friends you can trust. Without these base layers met, meeting your love and belonging needs can feel like a luxury you can't afford.

As you approach the top of Maslow's pyramid, you begin to look for intangible meaning, things such as recognition and approval. Maslow called this layer "esteem." As a younger person, that esteem often comes from others, but as you age, this need is more about self-esteem, dignity, independence, achievement, and mastery. You start to feel secure in who you are and less likely to need external validation for your self-worth.

The pinnacle of Maslow's pyramid is called "self-actualization." This means you live a life full of purpose and meaning. Am I important? Am I relevant to the world? Do people need me? Because your basic requirements are met, you have the freedom to seek personal growth and peak experiences. It's hard to worry about mastering your skills when you're starving, living in poverty, or trapped in an abusive relationship. For these reasons, you must deal with the lower levels of need before moving up to higher levels.

The bottom four levels of Maslow's hierarchy are all deficiency based, which means they're motivated by lack. You feel hungry because you haven't eaten. That's motivating! That hunger doesn't go away until you eat. If your basic needs are in question, it is difficult to think beyond them.

But the top layer, self-actualization, is different. Self-actualization is about recognizing and embracing your full potential. It's a growth need. Growth needs are always present and don't go away once you meet the basic level. The more you grow, the stronger these needs can become. This is freedom, which allows you to shift focus from fulfilling the fundamental necessities of life to living a life of significance and meaning.

My goal is to help you meet the lower-level needs of Maslow's pyramid successfully so that you can turn your attention to growth needs. To do this, you must first address the foundational Five Freedoms:

- Purpose

- Health

- Relationships

- Time

- Financial

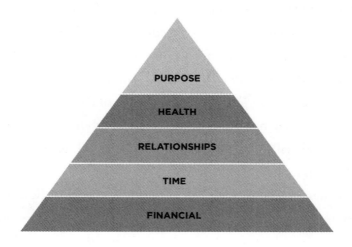

Like Maslow's Hierarchy of Needs, the Five Freedoms pyramid depicts the journey from dependency toward personal freedom.

The first step toward freedom is what most people think of: financial freedom. For the majority, financial freedom is the ultimate chase, and we have been taught not to expect it until the traditional retirement age, sometime in our sixties. This chase hinders movement to the other four freedoms until late in life, with many never fully realizing those other four freedoms. Having money does eliminate some of the barriers that block people from accessing their potential and can afford you peace and space to *be*, but as you will see, it is not the ultimate freedom.

Why do we all chase money? Usually it's because we actually want more time. You can't buy back time that has passed, but you can buy time today and going forward by having other people do things that you don't want to do or can't do well. It's a new way to think of currency, and this transaction can buy us more personal freedom.

Too often I hear people claim that if they just had financial freedom, their lives would be full. As you can see from the Five Freedoms pyramid, however, that is merely the starting point. There are many additional freedoms beyond financial freedom.

The next focus of the Five Freedoms is relationships. Freedom with relationships is about not having to deal with people that you don't want to deal with. This means not having to accept every patient who comes in just because you have to pay the bills. It could also mean not having to accept insurance reimbursement schedules. If you're financially free, you can make choices about who you hire and who you let go.

The next freedom often gets off-loaded—personal health. What do people do when they're stressed out? They typically eat poorly and avoid exercise. Many people ignore their health because they're so mired in the daily grind of keeping their head above water. How much is financial freedom worth if you have poor or limited health? Without this freedom, you are incapable of enjoying any of the other freedoms.

The top of the Five Freedoms pyramid is similar to Maslow's: what he calls self-actualization, I call purpose—legacy, significance, meaning. Sometimes when we're not financially free, money can feel like the finish line. What's your real purpose? What's your real meaning? What makes you significant? Until you can achieve the other freedoms, you may never have a chance to ponder, *What am I really about?* If you're a dentist, CPA, or engineer, those are great careers, but do they truly inspire you? Is there more? The answer is yes!

What people learn universally with age is that money is not the end goal. It's inspiring to observe this realization as our Freedom Founders members navigate their freedom journeys. The emotional and logical parts of their brains come together, and they realize how much they want to be significant and meaningfully contribute.

Once you have achieved financial freedom, more time, nourishing relationships, and a healthy body, you can consider your legacy and how you can share the freedom mindset with others. Furthermore, when Freedom Founders members achieve freedom and still want to make more money or grow an empire, it's because it's in their hearts. It's an innate passion that is their purpose.

When you are living at the top of the pyramid and playing to your strengths, life is incredibly rewarding. It's like living in your zone and having the luxury of pondering your purpose. You still have challenges, but you're able to face them with energy. You live life surrounded by people you enjoy. You love challenges and enjoy solving problems because you're not emotionally drained and physically depleted.

When you're operating at that level, you demand the best of yourself, knowing you can deliver. You do what you do because it's what you *want* to do and where you *want* to be. You're not a cog in a system that just doesn't fit you.

Life at the top of the Five Freedoms pyramid will look different for each person, and that's why it's important not to let society tell you what success looks like. That kind of well-intentioned positive peer pressure will hijack your life and keep you from finding your unique ability and living your purpose.

> That kind of well-intentioned positive peer pressure will hijack your life and keep you from finding your unique ability and living your purpose.

AN ALTERNATE APPROACH TO WORK AND WEALTH

Now that you understand *why* you aspire toward the top of the Five Freedoms pyramid, let's look at *how* you can get there. As we've mentioned, this requires a new mindset that embraces an alternate approach to work and wealth.

When Kandace and I work with new members (what is unique

about the Freedom Founders community is that our members attend and participate as couples), we start by finding their financial Freedom Number™—the monthly passive recurring cash flow needed to fund one's lifestyle derived from investments not directly tied to your labor (passive income being non-transactional income). Once Your Freedom Number is attained, you have choices and options to live and work as you wish—that's freedom.

When you're looking at where you want to go in life, it's essential to have a Freedom Number as your target because it covers your lifestyle burn rate—or the cash flow number that can provide for your lifestyle needs and wants. Note that the Freedom Number is *not* an accumulation number as espoused by the traditional financial planning model. The Freedom Number is a real number for which a firm target can be created, removing the uncertainty that the majority find unnerving when deciding if and when they can leave active income.

What if instead of spending your entire life working for money, you acquire capital assets, tangible assets such as real businesses and real estate that produce multiples of income with limited oversight required? Moreover, that recurring cash flow at some point replaces what you need to fund your lifestyle? And that passive income doesn't stop producing when you're not working? Also, passive income doesn't run out or become depleted over time? That's freedom.

Society has created its own version of freedom; it's called "retirement." Go to school, climb the educational ladder as high as possible to a career path, work for forty years, and then what? Retire? Good luck!

Society has it backward. The message is "work hard for forty years and then enjoy the fruits of your labor." Well, maybe—if the stock market doesn't crash and send you back to start over. If inflation doesn't destroy your nest egg before your time is up. If healthcare costs don't ruin your savings. If taxes and wealth redistribution policies don't strip away all your hard work and savings. If your health has not left you immobile or in some way disabled from full enjoyment of life.

The traditional financial model provided by Wall Street advisers goes like this: work, save, and turn your hard-earned capital over to money managers who will build you an "accumulation plan." As we discussed in chapter 1, this "advice" is misguided, however, and doesn't allow your wealth to work for you. Its basic premise is to accumulate the biggest pile of cash you can and then deplete principal out of that pile over several decades.

Note also that the traditional model never builds confidence or a firm plan over which the professional has any control. And that creates uncertainty and fear. But that's what Wall Street and society say is the right way to go. So the majority default and often realize the limitations only when it is too late.

The traditional method isn't about predictable cash flow. It's a dinosaur model based on saving, accumulating, and hoping that there is enough to last the rest of your life. What about inflation? The cost of living? Do you think that might change the accumulation model plan? Of course. This is why the traditional approach leaves people "shrinking toward retirement" only to live a downsized life in their later years. There's nothing golden about that!

Money is the exchange medium between wealth and that for which we want to trade. Wealth is only valuable as an exchange for cash, cash flow, or time. Otherwise, its value is only a guesstimate and is the reason the traditional financial model based on accumulation is flawed and leaves so many with gross uncertainty. So why do the majority fall for the traditional financial planning model? Because if your grandparents did it, your parents did it, and your colleagues do it, you probably will do it too.

While professionals are well educated in their specific fields, most never acquire more than essential financial acumen. Following the majority groupthink is the safe and the logical solution. And if it doesn't work out, at least you're in good company. Or are you?

With the freedom approach, on the other hand, you create sustainable passive cash flow. By knowing your Freedom Number, you know what capital asset amount is required to get you to your goal. Obviously, the lower your Freedom Number is, the faster you get to all of the additional Five Freedoms and break the chains from active income production.

One way to visualize the alternate approach to wealth is through the Freedom Curve™. It's the pathway to get to true freedom sooner in life than the traditional paths:

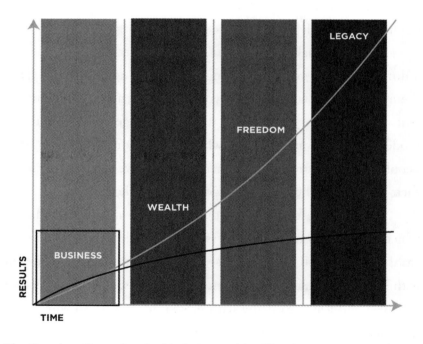

The Freedom Curve is a tool to help you identify where you currently are so you can find your own path to freedom.

Using a traditional career path, you would see a curve when you start your career and reach some level of success and income; from there, however, the line would plateau and stay relatively linear or stagnant until later years when it would start to decline.

Using the constructs presented in the following chapters, however, you'll experience acceleration bumps in the curve that I call "inflection points." These are leverage points—almost like trampolines—that propel you toward your Freedom Number.

Inflection points are like rip currents—they can take you under if you don't understand how to effectively use their momentum. Boaters who are skilled at navigating rip currents understand that if they are in the right place at the right speed, they can use the momentum of the current to get where they need to go exponentially faster.

So, too, can inflection points help you cover a lot of ground quickly. They help you reach your goal faster, as long as you remain aware of their presence and their potential. They're not something to fear; they're something to welcome. You just have to understand when and how to use them.

In the lower left of the Freedom Curve, you see the technician's practice or business. Most practitioners spend the majority of their focus on this area, trading their time for dollars. When I share the curve with clients, I stop and ask them to pinpoint where they are on the curve. Most people point to the practice vertical.

Since most people put their energy on the practice vertical, there is not much focus on the next vertical, wealth. This is when people rely on or abdicate too heavily on a traditional plan, like the 401(k). You may think that since you have a 401(k), you are technically building wealth and won't have to think about it. That's a huge mistake, because the big inflection point is right there at the junction of the practice box and the wealth vertical.

If you get your money working for you as hard as it potentially can without undue risk, then you've harnessed the power of the curve. If you stay with the traditional plan, which is abdicating your money to Wall Street financial advisers, you miss the inflection on that curve and remain stagnant and linear.

The point of the Freedom Curve is to help you self-assess where you are and how you can get to the next vertical. After wealth comes freedom, meaning you have wealth creating the financial freedom. From there, you can work though the Five Freedoms of health, relationships, time, and ultimately, to purpose or legacy.

Just as Maslow's hierarchy begins with a foundational piece, so does my freedom-based approach to work and wealth. Taking the time and effort to build a foundation for freedom can not only change your path from the traditional one to the antitraditional one; it can change your life and your future. I call this process the Freedom Assets, and it's one that all my clients follow.

By investing in the Freedom Assets, you can begin transitioning from a traditional path of wealth building to an alternative freedom-based approach. As we will explore fully in the following chapters, each asset is an essential foundational component on which to build your fullest, freest life.

FREEDOM ASSETS:

- Invest in Yourself
- Invest in Your Business
- Invest in Your Relationships
- Invest in Your Capital
- Invest in Your Legacy

Invest in Yourself

The first Freedom Asset is about developing and acquiring transferable skills and accumulated experiences that give you the ability to be adaptable and flexible. Considering that the global culture is moving at ever-growing speeds, changing entire industries almost overnight, it is more important now than ever to be malleable.

I don't care how carefully you plan your life—unexpected detours will happen. When these occur, being able to adapt or quickly reset can be the difference between survival and failure. By investing in yourself through acquired knowledge and skills, you are ensuring your viability and capability no matter what industry you choose. For this reason, I encourage all of my clients to continually foster their self-education in addition to their formal education.

It was through my own self-education that I began to understand how and why real estate made more sense as an investment strategy than the stock market. When my daughter's unexpected health issues arose, it was because of my decades of self-education that I had a backup plan I could confidently rely on—real estate.

It doesn't matter what your formal education looks like. In fact, you might not have any formal education, and that is fine. As we will learn in the next chapter, success is not dependent on the formal education process; it exists in spite of it. And as we'll learn in chapter 5, no degree will be able to give you the value of a mentor or coach. You don't have to go back to school to get an education; mentorships are a great place to begin your self-improvement. Start where you are.

Invest in Your Business

For several years after I started practicing dentistry, I was an associate dentist in another doctor's practice. This benefited me in a couple of ways: first, I wasn't ready to run a business at that point because I needed to develop clinical skills; second, it provided me the opportunity to stay involved in real estate. If I would've gone right into owning a practice, as many medical professionals do, there was a good chance I would not have had enough bandwidth to learn to invest in real estate at the same time—this is an example of a key inflection point in my own life.

After about three years, however, I started thinking more about running my own practice. If I'm being honest, my venture into owning a practice was mostly based on wanting more control. No matter my motives, I opened my own practice, and it was an exciting time. Having invested in my business gave me the foothold I needed to invest in real estate and ultimately find my way to freedom.

Invest in Your Relationships

For anyone interested in a freedom-based approach to work and wealth, it's important to get outside your own industry. Too many people limit their networks to their professional associations, societies, and club meetings. Everything is all inside the same small box. That's playing small. If you want to play big, you need to play in a bigger box.

As I know from experience, it's easy for highly trained, highly specialized individuals to stay within their small group of similar, like-minded peers. This is certainly a comfortable position, but it's not going to push you to fully express yourself and help you weather life's challenges.

It's invaluable to have people you can call who will give you unbiased, objective advice. I don't know where I would be without these networks. If I had maintained only my dentistry connections, then I would probably not have had the courage to sell my practice because those friends would have found the decision too risky. Since I also had a network of entrepreneurial investors, they encouraged me to think outside the norm and take a chance on freedom.

Building a Freedom Lifestyle™ is not a solo adventure. Force yourself, if you have to, but make the time and effort to get out and meet other people outside your field.

Invest in Your Capital

You should think of money as your employees. Your dollars should work as hard for you as you work for them. This is when self-education comes into play. If you don't study ways to make your money work, then you unconsciously follow the traditional path of saving.

How hard are your dollars working in a savings account today? Not very hard. How can you get your dollars to work more effectively? I make my dollars effective through real estate. No matter the source you choose, getting your money to work better for you is key to attaining financial freedom faster than you would otherwise.

Invest in Your Legacy

As a young person, my attention was on myself, my family, and my daughter's health. I wasn't really looking beyond taking care of what was immediately in front of me. As my daughter matured, I wondered how I might assist her in finding her own direction. For years, I wondered how I might give her, and other young people like her, guidance.

I didn't start thinking about legacy until I saw there was another way I could help people aside from being a dentist. When Freedom Founders organically started in 2010, I recognized I had created my next. When I was conducting interviews for my book *The Apprentice*

Model, I realized how much I could give back to young people by using my own story as a guide.

Once I found freedom and could create some space and objectivity, I started to see what in my life had worked and what hadn't. When I share my experiences, it especially resonates with young people. Reaching this group has given me purpose and meaning and has become the cornerstone of creating a legacy.

WHY SHARE MY STORY?

Freedom is doing what you want to do, when you want to do it, with whom you want to do it, and where you want to do it. This might conjure images of lying in a hammock on a pristine beach sipping fruity drinks with an umbrella, but that's not the point.

> Freedom is doing what you want to do, when you want to do it, with whom you want to do it, and where you want to do it.

Freedom means continuing to be relevant in whatever capacity you choose. It's about being significant and purposeful, creating a dent, and having influence. Freedom means keeping your power yourself rather than divvying it out to all the people and obligations who require something from you.

I am living my definition of freedom. I love what I do. I get to do it with people I enjoy. I get to travel and choose my schedule. I admit that I still do a lot, but it's because that's my choice. I feel compelled because I like doing it.

Oftentimes the lessons I share about financial education are the ones that hook people, but what we are offering is about so much more than just financial freedom. Just as Maslow's hierarchy of needs suggests, there is a lot more to life than the basic necessities, like personal fulfillment, evolution, and fully actualized potential. In sharing my story, the real message is about finding your own next and meeting your own needs.

The most effective way to connect with others is through stories. You can learn about a person's hopes and fears, priorities, and goals through their stories. They allow us to see one another as humans. Just because you may be a teacher or leader sharing your story does not mean you haven't experienced heartbreak, setbacks, or even downright failures.

When you are vulnerable and willing to share your story, you allow someone to see that success is never guaranteed or easy. It's always a challenge and a journey. The moment when a listener hears a hardship they too have experienced, that's when you've made a human connection.

This relationship between storyteller and listener has inspired me to continue sharing my story, with all its detours and setbacks along the way. Understanding the importance of investing in one's legacy has inspired me to share my experiences in articles, newsletters, books, and workshops and has become the foundation of Freedom Founders.

What is unique about Freedom Founders is that we recognize the value of human connection through the sharing of stories. For this reason, we create networks of people who can teach and inspire one another. Once a new member has met the community, then Kandace and I invite them to our home to continue the conversation and connect on a basic human level. We call these Freedom Blueprint Days.

When people meet Kandace, they're surprised to hear that she has a background in institutional finance. With a double major in accounting and finance, she sold stocks and mutual funds to institutions. When we met, she saw what I was doing with real estate and agreed it made a lot of sense.

She always tells our clients that she was skeptical until she invested her own money in some real estate opportunities that came through me. She tells clients, "I was always a stock person. I did energy stocks, and I had my own investments there, and I did okay. When I met David and saw what real estate could do, however, I realized it made more sense than using the financial market."

When clients come to meet with us (often as a couple) in our home, Kandace brings skills that I don't have. She is able to connect with people easily and has a knack for taking complex concepts and making them easily digestible. She is articulate, and people love to hear her talk because she gets right to the point. Her viewpoints empower our discussions, and I think her finance background reassures people that we have tried it all and have discovered the surest path to freedom.

When people see me and Kandace today, it's easy to assume we've had easy lives because we run a vibrant business. When they hear the struggles and challenges we overcame to get here, they start to fully embrace the possibility that they, too, can forge the same path to freedom. Through this communication, we hear members' stories change from strained admissions to hopeful musings about what their futures might hold.

I regularly post quick-hitting videos for those looking to jumpstart their freedom journey. Watch online at YouTube.com/User/DrDPhelps.

The people who are drawn to us are open to an alternative path. I see a common entrepreneurial thread in the people who are attracted to us. They are inspired by our story and the stories of other people who we've worked with who have taken antitraditional paths to achieve freedom.

Most of them have gone to school and achieved a certain level of success. Despite the varied professions and fields, however, they are all asking themselves, "What's my next?" They're not necessarily seeking the goal of retirement; they're seeking options and alternate ways of living their lives unshackled to work.

They understand that there are abstract needs that exist outside of finances and time. They are seeking growth needs and pondering how they might be the best version of themselves for their own sake and the sakes of their loved ones. True freedom is having the luxury of finances, time, relationships, and health to seek out the purpose, meaning, and significance you rightfully deserve.

TAKEAWAYS:

- Deficiency-based needs are motivated by a lack, fear, and scarcity mindset.
- Growth needs are always present and don't go away once you meet the basic needs.
- Your financial Freedom Number is the monthly passive income amount required to replace your active trading time for dollars income.
- The Freedom Curve is a self-assessment tool to help visualize the alternative approach, identify inflection points, and reach true freedom sooner in life than the traditional paths.

- There is more to life than meeting the basic necessities. Strive for personal fulfillment and evolution and recognizing your fully actualized potential.

CHAPTER 3

Invest in Yourself

I'm eight years old, perched on the top stair of my family home. From this familiar vantage point, I can hear my parents' conversations about the fascinating inner workings of the grown-up world I have yet to join.

Tonight my father is talking to my mother in a tight voice. This is the voice he always uses when he talks about his "investment deals." This one apparently involved a Florida orange grove: "The whole grove froze! Froze!" I hear my mother comforting him in hushed tones, though his frustrated sighs continue. I don't know what "investing" means, but it's clear my dad lost money doing something he doesn't fully understand.

My dad is a smart, successful, prudent man, but some of his investment deals don't work out so well. He knows that he needs to do something different, but he has no guidance and no community—no board of advisers. How can I improve on this when I'm a grown-up? How can I find something that I understand and have more control over than fruit growing halfway across the country?

■ ■ ■

A friend of mine, Richard, has a twenty-one-year-old son in college named Michael. Like his father, Michael has an entrepreneurial spirit. While attending college, he started an online web development business that is already making a revenue. Because of Michael's early entrepreneurial acumen and his father's proven entrepreneurial successes, I invited them both to talk with me for the *Dentist Freedom Blueprint* podcast.

During our conversation, I asked Michael about the adult conversations he might have overheard from the top of the proverbial stairs that informed his mindset. He explained that he did overhear those conversations and always tried to participate in them: "I found them interesting whether it was business talk, management talk, whatever it was. I believe those conversations shaped my journey and provided a foundational understanding of entrepreneurship from the beginning."

In his younger years, Michael experimented with businesses— from selling lemonade to mowing lawns. Once he became interested in computers, he started teaching computer classes to senior citizens. In doing this, he saw an opportunity to put his training resources online, so he created a YouTube channel. When he hit fifty subscribers, he built a website for the channel. Being young and ambitious, he tested different web development platforms and landed on one he liked that was new and therefore didn't have training materials. This gave him the idea to pioneer that training content.

Not long after, the platform grew as well as his training channel. He was soon contacted by an entrepreneur to do the same thing for their website, and one client led to the next. Now his channel has reached over 27,000 subscribers and gets more than 120,000 views a month. He has seven employees and currently boasts a web development business with an annual revenue of $150,000 that helps transform entrepreneurs' ideas into realities.

When I asked his father, Richard, how he fostered his son's entrepreneurial mindset, he explained that he and his wife didn't force entrepreneurialism; they merely made space for it:

> *When you discover a young person in your family or in your circle who's got an entrepreneurial spirit, there are responsibilities on both sides. Your responsibility as a mentor is to be able to show them the right way and help them with the expertise that you have. Their responsibility is to implement what they learn. And to Michael's credit, he is one of the most rapid implementers that I have ever met in my career, and I've worked with some really amazing people.*

Obviously, Michael is not the traditional college student. "I just think differently," he admits. "Personally, I thrive on being different. I like to be different. But does it become tough sometimes to balance friends, girlfriend, school, fraternity, all of these things and run a business? Yes, it certainly does at times. I find ways to balance it, but it can be difficult."

Many of my Freedom Founders clients are highly specialized with copious amounts of education and training. Michael, on the other hand, represents the renegade young person who is questioning the traditional path that so many people trod with little thought. That doesn't mean he won't choose it ultimately, but he is attempting to make an informed decision that leads him to a freer future. "I know what society thinks," he says, "that the right path is to attend college, get a bachelor's degree, and then try to make a lot of money. That's the traditional path, and I think that deviating from that's not always a bad thing."

Michael could do anything he wants, but instead, he's testing to see what else is out there: "Just because I'm in school right now doesn't mean all I do is learn the traditional things they teach me and that's it. I'm constantly learning outside of school. Constantly searching for new business techniques, talking with people, reading blogs, and watching videos to improve myself and my business. You have to constantly learn and then at some point put it into play."

Michael has learned what it takes most people decades, if not lifetimes, to learn: that success is less about being smart and more about weathering challenges, experiencing trial and error, figuring out what works, being nimble and adaptable, and finding ways to invest in the first Freedom Asset—yourself.

To hear more of my discussions with thought leaders like Richard and Michael, subscribe to the *Dentist Freedom Blueprint* podcast at DentistFreedomBlueprint.com.

WHY SHOULD I INVEST IN MYSELF?

Most children pursue their curiosities with enthusiasm and optimism. When they're asked what they'd like to be when they grow up, their answers are usually definitive: *Astronaut! Bigfoot researcher! The Easter bunny!* If you ask someone who is Michael's age the same question, you rarely get the same enthusiasm or certainty: Dentist? Maybe a teacher? Something in tech? When do we lose our zeal for choosing what's next? Where does our audacity go, and why do our answers becomes so serious and pragmatic?

Children naturally follow what interests them; adults follow what *should* interest them. This isn't merely an innate shift—it's also validated by well-meaning adults. In my case, I stopped exploring partly because I showed some early academic aptitude. Rather than follow my musings, I was suddenly expected to read, learn, test, repeat.

> ## Children naturally follow what interests them; adults follow what *should* interest them.

I was unknowingly set on a path toward achievement. I lost my tendency to explore because I was fearful that if I deviated from the path laid before me, it might distract me, and I wouldn't be deemed "good" in the eyes of my teachers, family, and mentors. With the expectations placed on me, I felt like I had to put all my time and effort into a traditional career path.

Positive attention garnered for showing aptitude oftentimes pigeonholes young people. It makes them think they must become highly skilled and specialized to be successful or meet the expectations of the adults around them. We've all done it unknowingly each time we ask a bright-eyed child, "What do you want to be when you grow up?" This question reinforces the relationship between aptitude and expected achievement.

The whole construct of today's broad educational system—from kindergarten, grade school, middle school, high school, to advanced degrees—teaches you how to be a good worker at different levels rather than demonstrating how to make money. Formal education is missing so many pieces of practical application to life. No matter what field you go into, without sensible knowledge of business, budgeting, investment, and the compounding of debt versus the compounding of investments, the income earned will not compound and lead to a Freedom Lifestyle.

A NOTE FOR PARENTS, TEACHERS, AND MENTORS:

How can adults in leadership roles foster the important skill of self-investment in young people? Though some adults are bound by curricula and teaching frameworks, the most profound lessons adults can pass to children are those that deal with leadership, critical thinking, conflict resolution, character building, collaboration, and emotional intelligence. Reminding young people that these are tools for success that aren't found in textbooks allows them to alter their mindset and seek out these opportunities to begin self-educating early.

Also, by not making the achievement—the championship, the test, the degree—the pinnacle of success, you allow youth to appreciate the process rather than just the product. There's considerable value in exploring and learning that the achievement itself never offers. If mentors can incorporate the bigger picture, then they are offering an alternate construct that can greatly benefit young people.

Lastly, when you see a young person ignited by a concept or a field of study, take the opportunity to mirror their enthusiasm: "Wow, you really seem to be excited about exploring nature," or, "I can tell by your enthusiasm that collaborative projects really enliven you." This subtle strategy helps the young person begin to see the totality of who they are outside their achievements and "accepted" interests.

Lastly, encourage the youth with whom you interact. Even if they mess up or veer off course, celebrate the tenacity they demonstrate by merely sticking with the journey and continuing to show up. Through these subtle strategies, you can give young people a powerful advantage on their own paths to freedom.

For more information on how to advise and cultivate the emerging leaders in your life, see my book *The Apprentice Model: A Young Leader's Guide to an Anti-Traditional Life*.

There is of course a need for formalized education, but it doesn't have to come through the constructs we use today. Even though society traditionally stresses formal education as the answer, I don't believe that it is. What is the answer? Self-education.

Many of the most successful people have taken self-education and made it the cornerstone of their training. There are numerous examples of prosperous individuals without high-level educations—Abraham Lincoln, Thomas Edison, Henry Ford, Steve Jobs, Oprah Winfrey, Bill Gates, Michael Dell, and Mark Zuckerberg, to name a few. As these individuals have proven, formal education is not a precursor to success.

There are always limitations to any education system, which is why the first and most important investment in a Freedom Lifestyle is yourself. For this reason, the first Freedom Asset I teach is to invest in yourself.

Investing in yourself means exploring ideas, topics, and subjects independent of the requisite curriculum of your formal education. This includes everything outside of what's required to pass tests. Investing in yourself means acquiring skills and learning practical strategies for conflict resolution, collaboration, emotional intelligence, and human connection.

People who excel in life often do it, not *because* of their formal education but *in spite* of it. They've learned these soft skills somewhere outside of traditional training. Most successful people have created lifestyles that allow them to be inspired by other people from a variety of fields. This provides them with well-rounded intellects that make them more adaptable, flexible, and resourceful people than those who focused their mental energies on one specialized field.

Speaker and author Jim Rohn is well known for saying, "Formal education will make you a living; self-education will make you a fortune." Though the definition of "fortune" can be debated, his point is that we all have blind spots. The effort and attention you give to filling in those areas develop skills that make you a more resilient and adaptive person—two essential traits in any entrepreneur.

Success is not based on grades, achievements, or dollars; it's based on the commitment to continual learning. In formal education there's a tendency to make the achievement itself—the graduation, the licensed degree, the certificate, the job—be the end goal. That is limiting, because that achievement only opens one door to one opportunity. If you don't continue to self-educate, to self-improve, throughout life, then that's the only door you have.

Investing in yourself is about unlocking more doors. In this way, you are not limited to one specialty. It often reminds me of the Choose Your Own Adventure book series. When you're highly specialized, you have one option for an ending. Imagine being thirty years old and knowing exactly how the rest of your life will look! Depressing, right? Whereas the more you invest in yourself, the more options you add. You're essentially creating multiple endings for yourself.

The whole point of building a life and asking yourself "What's my next?" is to ensure you have more than one door ahead of you at all times. If there is only one door before you, there's no reason to question your next, because the only option is "what is." That's the problem I observe in my new clients—they get to the point in their careers when they have to quit practicing because their bodies or spirits are spent, and they realize there are no other doors, no other options. Why? Because they forgot to invest in the first Freedom Asset—themselves.

Self-education is about creating an environment for yourself where you can absorb information and experiences from other sources. Thanks to the digital age, it's easy to seek out resources that spark your curiosity and fill the voids of your formal education. Self-education comes from books, lectures, online resources, podcasts, and videos.

Apprentice model experiences with thought leaders can also be powerful ways to self-educate. Such opportunities can help you gain a different perspective on work and wealth and can propel you toward a Freedom Lifestyle. (See my suggestions for self-education tools in the Resources and Our Services sections at the end of the book.)

Many professionals spend so much time and energy learning specialized skills that they atrophy in other ways. Simply by expanding your knowledge base through resources on self-development, finance, leadership, investing, and more, you expand your interests and inclinations outside your profession. In addition to piquing your interests in other areas, this simple strategy gives you permission to explore other fields and find what you've been missing.

This tactic often leads to reinvigoration about themes and subjects that have gone dormant for too long because of the demands of traditional education and professional development. This begins to alter how you think about yourself, who you are, and what your next might be. Oftentimes my clients report childish delight and wonder when they step outside their traditional boxes and allow themselves to explore the world and networks around them.

Furthermore, exploration not only leads to new discoveries about your external world; it leads to powerful understandings about your internal world. Self-awareness is an underrated yet highly valuable asset on the journey toward personal and financial freedom. In order to know what your next is, you need to know what provides you energy and what saps it. Self-awareness is the starting point for investing in yourself. Once you are aware of what ignites you, then you can pursue those interests with zeal.

> In order to know what your next is, you need to know what provides you energy and what saps it. Self-awareness is the starting point for investing in yourself.

Comparative mythologist Joseph Campbell considered these individual interests as the gateways to contentment. In *The Power of Myth*, he asserts, "If you do follow your bliss you put yourself on a kind of track that has been there all the while, waiting for you, and the life that you ought to be living is the one you are living."[1] As Campbell understood, these innate interests often hold the key to unlocking your full potential and meaning.

The first step to investing in yourself is knowing yourself and what excites and ignites you. Once you can recognize your "bliss," seek it boldly. As Campbell encourages, "Any life career that you choose in following your bliss should be chosen with that sense— that nobody can frighten me off this thing. And no matter what happens, this is the validation of my life and action."[2]

Learning more about who you are through new social networks and resources can provide you a road map of what excites you—your

---

1   Joseph Campbell, *The Power of Myth* (New York: Doubleday, 1988), 120, 190.

2   Campbell, 120, 190.

bliss—and take you one step closer to your full potential. It sounds simple, but it's imperative that you think more about who you are outside of what you do. If we lived in a culture that asked, "So, who are you?" rather than, "So, what do you do?" then we might make strides toward changing this mindset and toward understanding that self-awareness is integral to happiness and success.

Self-awareness allows you to give your innate interests space to grow into new opportunities and alternate options. Within them lie the answers to "What's my next?" When you are unaware of the totality of your personality, you risk latent attributes suffocating. Once you start exploring, however, you can discover new doors, or new nexts.

Typically, once I encourage my clients to follow their intrinsic curiosities, they become voracious self-investors and self-educators quickly. With each new resource, they are investing in their greatest asset—themselves—and adding new options should they need or want them in the future.

Exploration through self-improvement and self-investing allows you to put yourself in different environments than your primary one. As I was writing this chapter, I attended a conference on the topic of people who had taken their primary skill set and magnified it in some way. One of the keynote speakers—an entrepreneurial dentist who owns multiple practices—said, "No dentist wants his tombstone's epitaph to read, *I was a dentist.*" This is a succinct (and morbid) reminder that your skills are not your legacy. No matter if you were the greatest dental provider that ever lived, is that leaving any kind of legacy to others? Does that skill fulfill you completely?

Typically, your identity is linked to how resourceful, resilient, and secure you feel. This self-identity has everything to do with how we think and behave. Self-investing gives us a more creative and adaptive mindset, which is often the precursor to success. Let your career be your foothold to get you the life to which you aspire. Allow life to be full of what excites you, interests you, fills you up, and challenges you.

Getting to know yourself better and investing in your uniqueness can be a transformative experience. Though this self-exploration is often lauded in children, it can be squashed in adults. I'll admit it can be intimidating at first, especially for someone in the habit of trading time for dollars because it can feel like a waste of time.

Give yourself encouragement while you work to change this mindset. Time spent investing in yourself is not a waste; it's asset building, and it is the foundation upon which a Freedom Lifestyle is built. Don't judge where you are or what your interests are. Just trust the curiosities and then show up for yourself.

SHOWING UP

In *My Unfinished Business*, my mentor, Dan Kennedy, talks about the conversations that young children overhear from the top of their stairs. He notes that many successful people he has met recall overhearing positive messages, whereas others who received more mixed or negative messages have to "work hard at un-doing and replacing that 'unprosperous' programming, some acknowledging they still catch it inhibiting them even today."[3]

What Kennedy notes—and many of us have lived—is that our entrepreneurial mindsets are often passed to us in our formative years by the adults in our lives. These early experiences can shape how we show up for ourselves and how easily we can invest in ourselves in our adult years.

---

3   Dan Kennedy, *My Unfinished Business* (Charleston: Advantage Media, 2009), 23.

When I was a young boy sitting at the top of the stairs listening to my parents discuss the most recent investment opportunity gone bad, I unknowingly began drafting my blueprint for a Freedom Lifestyle. Even though my father was the model of a creative, persistent investor, he wasn't always an informed one. I was fascinated by the financial freedom he nobly pursued, but I made a vow to myself during those eavesdropping sessions that I would be in control of my life and my finances. There would be no citrus groves on the other side of the country for me!

When I was a teenager, my dad took me along on a visit to his financial adviser. He and my father discussed penny stocks, and before leaving, my dad agreed to invest in them. Like the frozen oranges, this turned out to be another failed investment. This time it was because my dad took advice from someone he assumed knew the market well. In reality, the adviser was making commission on the penny stocks and therefore gave biased advice.

I remember thinking, *If you aren't informed and don't have trusted guides, then you might as well be gambling.* I realized that investments can be purely speculative unless you are intentional about the process. I understood that if I was going to embark on my own investment journey, I would need to understand the terrain before I started my journey. I also needed to have guides I could trust.

In both my early entrepreneurism and my burgeoning career focus, my goal was to make money. I wondered, though, if there was a way to make my money work for me. It made sense that if I figured out a formula early, my life would be less stressful and afford more choices. In an effort to discover such strategies, I started reading books about the stock market and real estate during college. At this point, I didn't have any money to invest. I was like every other young adult I knew—I was waiting tables trying to keep my college debt down.

Thinking back, I can say that I was attempting to bring back the entrepreneurial side that had been squashed during my years of formal education. My self-education fueled my alter ego. Though I was focused on training for dentistry by day, I was learning about investments by night.

When I compared real estate investments versus more traditional modes of investment—stocks, bonds, annuities, mutual funds—real estate made the most sense. It also seemed a lot more reliable than the strategies my father had tried. It was an investment asset that I could exert some level of control over (and remember, I am all about control).

Real estate books led me to ones about finance, which led me to resources on budgeting and self-improvement. Once I started practicing dentistry, which I enjoyed, I still looked forward to coming home and opening a book or listening to a cassette tape (remember those?). These authors and thought leaders quickly became my mentors. I felt limitless with options spread before me. I no longer felt pigeonholed as I had during my educational years, but I still didn't see any way to leave my career to pursue my alter ego's burgeoning entrepreneurship.

As I found my "mentors," I subscribed to their mailing lists and newsletters. Soon, I started attending their seminars and lectures. I built a network of people who were outside the dental industry. They challenged me and thrilled me with new possibilities on how to make money. I felt less pressure to trade my time for dollars indefinitely. I intuited there was an alternate path than the traditional one modeled for me by my family and peers, but I just had to figure out how to find it.

As I continued investing in myself and chasing my interests in real estate investments, I became more confident and informed. By this point, my father and I sold the first investment property we'd purchased during college, so I had $25,000 in capital. I decided to use the profit and purchased another property. I'll get more into the specifics of these transactions in later chapters, but as I continued to learn and show up for myself, my investment portfolio grew.

As years passed and my dentist practice and family grew, I felt the stress of being a provider and the entrapment of being tied to my practice. It was Jenna's health issues that finally gave me the confidence to close one door and open a new one.

I decided to sell my practice, which wasn't an easy process, as I will discuss in later chapters. My first attempt failed miserably, and I had to go back in and revitalize what was then a failing practice. I did a lot of self-education in marketing, which allowed me to proceed with the sale as a more informed party. On my second attempt to sell the practice, I succeeded. I was free. But did I stop investing in myself? Never.

After I had left dentistry for the final time, I knew I was not going back. I admit that I felt a void, though I used that space to continue my self-exploration. During my education into marketing, I found resources that ignited my interest in being a better communicator. This led to materials about public speaking.

Let me be clear, I had never done public speaking. In fact, I never really thought about public speaking because it was far outside the dental industry. Something about being a better communicator, however, seemed important for all facets of my life. I didn't really have a reason why, but as I had learned from experience, I needed to recognize what interested me—my bliss—and then show up. So, that's what I did, and that's what I continue to do.

Safety for me is being in control. I don't want to give the false impression that my self-education, or yours, will be easy. In fact, sometimes what interests you is outside your comfort zone. (I learned this years later when I decided to learn how to dance. It wasn't easy or pretty, but I showed up, and now I can do a mean rumba!) Public speaking terrified me. I knew I wouldn't be in control. People might laugh at me. I may say something stupid. There were a million ways it could go wrong. But something in me was undeterred. I knew it was time to show up.

Looking back, it was the courage to show up at a public speaking course that was the first step on a journey that would lead to Freedom Founders. I'm not finished evolving, however; I continue to invest in myself because it's the greatest asset I have. There is a beginning of the self-investing journey, but there is no end. It's an ongoing evolution, and it can lead you to the most dynamic, evolved version of yourself.

My identity is no longer fragmented—my ego identifies as a dentist and my alter ego as a real estate investor. I am now the totality of these parts. I feel free, whole, myself. I want the same for all my clients and for the next generation.

When I counsel young people, I tell them they need to expose themselves to many fields and thought processes to avoid pigeonholing themselves to one specialty. Had I not been making fear-based decisions in my youth, I might have found out earlier that I love teaching, speaking, and authoring. Because of choosing a traditional path, however, I focused on one discipline and never deviated. Though this may have made me a more adept dental technician, it did not make me a more evolved human.

Oftentimes it's the fear of failure that starts people on a traditional path. Even though I had an early interest in entrepreneurism, I was too afraid to pursue it. I could fail; it was, therefore, too risky. This mindset kept me back and put many of my passions and skills on the back burner at my own detriment. It wasn't until I began investing in myself that my entrepreneurial fire was reignited. Luckily, I continued to stoke it, and it was burning bright when I made the bold decision to change my path and become Free for Life.

As I shared with Michael during our podcast interview, I am a huge advocate for young people taking time off between high school and college and then again between college and any graduate work. Breaks allow you to become aware of your interests. They give you opportunities to assess the doors ahead of you and make informed decisions about the best ones to open. Time off should be intentional and purposeful—not an excuse to party and couch surf. It is an opportunity to claim your path.

Choosing a traditional career path is fine *if it's your choice*. When you are passive, you are like a tumbleweed in the wind. You have no authority over your own life. The "in-between" phases in life—between schooling, jobs, children, relationships—are powerful opportunities to find yourself and uncover your next. By taking advantage of the in-between phases, you can explore options and make better decisions that get you the freedom to which you aspire. The trap would be to go into a field because that's what your parents, teachers, or mentors did or what you overheard from the top of the stairs.

To discover your own next, you have to be willing to be different and go against the norm. This takes courage. When you have taken time to become informed, however, you mitigate the risks of whatever endeavor you choose. As I learned from watching my own father, unless you understand the game and know how to play, investments can be as uncertain as gambling. Taking the time to self-invest makes each financial decision you make more sound and therefore more potentially advantageous.

There's nothing wrong with having a career or profession, something you like to do to help people or make a product or service. But how can you build a different life? You don't necessarily have to go to college or professional school to have a great life if that's not what you're set up to do. By reading this book and being aware of your own blind spots and limiting mindsets, you can compensate for any gaps.

Let this book be your permission to appreciate whatever education you have—formal or informal—and supplement it with areas that interest you. Self-education allows you to fill in gaps in your own education to ensure that you are resourceful, resilient, creative, and innovative.

I feel a self-imposed responsibility to take the lessons that I've learned in life and relay those—not to have you be like me, but to show you that you do have choices and options in life. Some young people might naively assume that success is a straight journey. Spoiler alert: it's not! You must accept that. But you don't have to let that be your downfall.

Investing in yourself enables you to weather the unpredictable, though guaranteed, storms. Self-exploration makes you more resilient for situations that you cannot plan for, as I learned firsthand from Jenna's health crises. If I had not spent decades investing in myself and acquiring skills outside of dentistry, I would have had one option when Jenna was sick—keep working and forgo more time with her. What a terrible position to be in, and yet countless professionals are put into it every day.

If there are things that you can do now to alleviate that pressure *someday*, then you should do them. Even if you're young and feeling invincible, trust those of us who have gone before and believe that the day will come when you are in a crisis. Investing in yourself is the thing that you can do now to weather those storms later. Being resourceful and adaptable is your best insurance policy.

I get excited about seeing young people like Michael who are sensing early in their lives that there are alternate paths to wealth and work. I want to empower that thinking and encourage people to embrace it. Schooling is a great option as long as you continue to supplement it with self-education so that you can shift, move, and iterate as you go.

You can certainly stay focused on one path, but what many young people I mentor today are understanding is that all careers require adapting rather than evolving. Evolution takes decades or generations; adaptation, on the other hand, is quick and timely and allows people to adjust more rapidly. Not only does adaptation ready a young person to stay viable in our fast-paced culture, but it creates a mindset of fluid adaptability that can afford them the career they want and the lifestyle they seek.

It's time to move beyond the trope of having one career path that's highly specialized because it doesn't allow for much movement. When you approach your career in this way, you end up spending your time and money on one skill set. Though it is admirable to be as proficient as possible, it's a linear improvement. You may learn some things and become a more efficient provider, but it will not affect your ability to earn more income. It is not getting you any closer to a Freedom Lifestyle.

We do need highly trained, specialized individuals; we need engineers, rocket scientists, doctors. There's nothing wrong with specialization. The problem is that most people continue to focus only on that skill set in an effort to improve their lives. A brain surgeon, for example, might spend another decade outside of school in residency and training programs. By the time they are "skilled" and ready to earn money and pay back student loans, they are already burned out and saddled by exponential debt. It doesn't have to be this way.

Though we need specializations, there must be a corollary path—or a plan B—of building additional skill sets that diversify people. Otherwise, we are continually neglecting the emotional debt paid by these highly skilled individuals. Being Free for Life is not just about financial freedom—it's about having the freedom to be fully engaged and present in a life that brings joy and fulfillment. It's about having the freedom to continue human development and actualization through continual self-investing.

TAKEAWAYS:

- Children naturally follow what interests them; adults follow what *should* interest them.

- People who excel in life often do not *because* of their formal education but *in spite* of it.

- Success is not based on grades, achievements, or dollars; it's based on the commitment and the willingness and permission to test and fail to learn.

- Self-exploration not only leads to new discoveries about your external world; it leads to powerful understandings about your internal world.

- To discover "What's your next?" you have to be willing to be different and go against the norm. This takes courage. When you have taken time to become informed, however, you mitigate the risks of whatever endeavor you choose.

CHAPTER 4

Invest in Your Business

Too many dentists, doctors, and professionals fail to create any investment income outside of their practice revenues. The problem with that is there is never any true freedom. Once we stop working, the cash flow also stops. David has an amazing passive real estate investment program that is helping professional practice owners build a real freedom retirement plan without being a landlord.

—Dr. Jim Rachor

David understands the struggles that dentists go through because he's gone through them himself. His service to his colleagues comes from a place of compassion and authenticity. I can't even begin to describe the value that he packs into his Freedom Founders Mastermind Group events. You have to see it to believe it.

—Dr. David J. Maloley

■ ■ ■

Dr. Paul is a new doctor with a young family. He discovered Freedom Founders several years ago while researching an alternative approach to wealth building. He started his career practicing as an associate doctor, meaning he didn't own the business but was paid as an employee in the practice.

Like many practitioners, he seeks his own business, yet he's wise enough to know he should learn the fundamentals of proprietorship first. He contacted me seeking advice about running a business, how to invest, and how to build capital assets to provide the passive revenue that would eventually set him free.

There will always be outliers who perceive things differently or are happy exploring. These people know there's more learning beyond what they received in school, and by golly, they're going to go uncover it. Dr. Paul is one of these people.

By joining Freedom Founders, Dr. Paul purposely put himself in an environment where he knew he'd be challenged about his thought processes. In this way, he proved himself an outlier. He positioned himself in a community where he could glean knowledge and wisdom from other people, while most of his medical peers were content with the status quo, maintaining a short-term mindset focused on one or two years ahead. Paul, on the other hand, was looking forward— way forward. He was planning for the inevitable professional and personal challenges, but he was also preparing for unforeseen opportunities as well.

Many young professionals follow the same path as Paul: they work hard in school, graduate, and accumulate debt in the process. Because it's too difficult to start a practice right away, many start as associates. Later, they often transition from being an employee in someone else's practice to owning their own. This is one of those in-between moments that I discussed in chapter 3.

Taking some time to consider what makes a "real" business and how to set it up can make or break your transition to a Freedom Lifestyle. It's an inflection point—one that provides large gains. You either hit the inflection point, leverage key elements, and lead your business into a dynamic new practice, or you miss the opportunity and maintain linear, minimal improvement and encounter many challenges ahead.

> Taking some time to consider what makes a "real" business and how to set it up can make or break your transition to a Freedom Lifestyle.

As a diligent beginner, Paul is growing his active income, though he wisely sought advice on how to invest in his medical practice in pursuit of achieving independence sooner. He views his business as an investment that can grow wealth and achieve freedom. Paul realizes that owning a practice can provide him a foothold—if it is done wisely.

If I can get other young people like Dr. Paul who want to have an enterprise or a business to start thinking about what a "real" business means, then they can begin working toward the next Freedom Asset—investing in their business.

A NOTE ON DEBT:

In our society, we have become almost immune to the debt load. It's normalized in a way that is damaging. When we couple the ease of accessing credit and loans with the human weakness of desire, it creates a devastating problem. Too much debt becomes a burden that some people never overcome.

I'd like to make the important distinction between good debt and bad debt. Bad debt is lifestyle consumption debt outside a home (unless you have overbought your home, in which case, that's bad debt). Financing cars, trips, and vacation homes is bad debt. You should pay off bad debt as quickly as possible.

Good debt, on the other hand, is using the proper financing to build and/or acquire capital assets, which equal real businesses and/or real estate. The only way to start out as a business owner is to use good debt. Furthermore, good debt can also be used to invest in yourself through education, but you must be discerning of how much debt you are assuming.

So many people are hard workers who avoid overspending. After years of this grind, however, you can start to feel a void. You don't know your hobbies; you don't know what enriches you because you are too consumed by the daily grind. We all can get fixated on extravagant vacations, cars, and homes, and when we work so hard, we can use our sacrifice as a means to justify our extravagances. We're depleted and hope things might fill us back up.

This starts a cycle of overspending to fill the void created by overworking, then overworking to pay off the overspending. Be aware that oftentimes the spending cycle begins when you choose to consume in an effort to enrich.

Remain cognizant of this deficit spending cycle so that when you feel the urge to consume, you can instead give yourself things that will actually enrich you—like time in nature, time with a loved one, or time alone enjoying your favorite hobby. There are many ways to fill yourself up without maxing out your finances. Change your consumption habits today to ensure a freer tomorrow.

ARE YOU A TECHNICIAN OR A BUSINESS OWNER?

Like Paul, many people who own a business or professional practice do so because they don't want to be employed by anybody; they want to be the employer and the boss. Owning a business comes with myriad burdens and is a competitive environment. Ownership requires that professionals, in addition to their technical skills, understand profit margins; cash flow; rapidly changing technologies and modalities; and the high cost of capital, risks, loans, and marketing.

Throw out the old practice models, as they are completely irrelevant today. With few exceptions, gone are the days of the solo doctor opening up a new practice and being deluged with patients, making a lot of money, and not having the foggiest idea how a real business should run. Fifty years ago, simply concentrating on good service was all that was necessary.

Dentistry and all of healthcare are being rapidly socialized, and in so doing, commoditized. It's a business that requires marketing and management skills. Managed care insurance now controls the future by dictating reimbursement rates and reducing the profit margins of the dental practice. At the same time, overhead costs are up along with massive government bureaucratic regulation. Any money left over (actual profit) to the dentist owner is being taxed at higher rates and will only increase in the future. In short, the solo practice is on a slippery slope.

To compete and remain private, today's dentist must operate a practice as a real business with similar systems and efficiencies as the corporate model. Maintaining independence will likely mean expanding hours of availability and employing associate doctors. Done well, an enterprising dentist could focus more time on the business of dentistry and perform the dentistry on their terms, or none at all.

All of these challenges mean that a person starting a business has a lot more to learn and manage without the help of a human resources company. Though an owner's motivations may be noble and forward thinking, most find that running a small business often becomes the small business running the owner. This is because the owner tries to do it all and becomes overworked and overburdened. When this happens, you don't own a business; you have bought and built yourself a job. In that way, you are self-employed because the business controls you.

When I talk about being a business owner, I'm not talking about being an overworked technician in a building you own; I'm talking about owning a real business. Many clients like Paul have asked what makes a real business. I always ask, "If you took three months off and went to Fiji with your family, would the business still exist when you return? Would it have money in the bank? Would you have gotten paid?" If you answer yes, then, congratulations—you have a real business. If you answer no, then you're essentially operating as a technician within your company, and you still have work to do building a real business.

If you want to own a real business, that doesn't mean you can't work there or invest your time and expertise, but you do need to be honest about who or what is in control. This small distinction makes all the difference when it comes to building your freedom.

The fast track model to freedom is transitioning from the sacrifice period of trading time for dollars to passive (or annuitized) income not solely dependent on the owner's active labor. Freedom is a transition from being the doer (technician) to the manager (self-employed) to a real business owner (entrepreneur).

In *The E-Myth Revisited*, author Michael Gerber distinguishes between technician and owner. He says, "The technical work of a business and a business that does that technical work *are two totally different things!*"[4] Though many people unknowingly enter entrepreneurship as a step toward freedom, they are actually further cementing themselves to the business's success. Gerber says, "Rather than being their greatest single asset, knowing the technical work of their business becomes their greatest single liability."[5]

Many young people learn this entrepreneurial lesson early when the skills that once invigorated them suddenly become one of many tedious responsibilities weighing on them. As Gerber asserts, "The business that was supposed to free him from the limitations of working for somebody else actually enslaves him. … Suddenly, an entrepreneurial dream turns into a technician's nightmare."[6] More seasoned professionals might not realize they are ensnared until it's time to retire, and that's when they realize they are so integral to the business that it can't function without them.

---

4   Michael Gerber, *The E-Myth Revisited: Why Most Small Businesses Don't Work and What to Do about It* (New York: HarperCollins, 2001), 13–14.

5   Gerber, 13–14.

6   Gerber, 13–14.

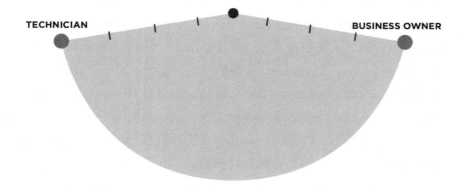

TECHNICIAN   BUSINESS OWNER

Where are you on the pendulum? Are you a technician or business owner? Understanding the difference could be the key to unlocking your Freedom Lifestyle.

Using the simple visual of a pendulum, you can discern what type of business you own. On one end of the spectrum, you have the technician. Here, everything is clinical and focused on doing the "thing." On the other side is the business owner not doing any of the operations.

Consider a McDonald's franchise owner: they are not on site managing people and flipping burgers. The real owner is not doing any operations at all. They do not need to be there for the business to function.

Most small businesses are self-employed jobs. Having the awareness that it doesn't have to be that way is the first step to changing it. Once you have the awareness about whether your role is of technician or business owner, that's the turning point, the opportunity to take action and become one step closer to a Freedom Lifestyle.

You have to decide where you want to be. There's no right or wrong. If you love being the technical operator of the thing, then focus on that, but understand you have to surround yourself with other people who can run the business side. If you are seeking freedom and discover that you are ensnared by the operations of your business, then you need to get real about how to transition out of that. There is another way.

Don't get discouraged if you are a technician; know that wherever you are now may evolve over time. Start where you are with a new awareness of the path to freedom. Think of what your ideal proportion of technician and business owner might be, and then reverse engineer to where you are. Figure out what steps you need to take now to get to your goal on that pendulum.

Once you have an objective awareness of your business, you have the opportunity to rebuild (or build) your business so that it is a real one that provides a foothold on your path to freedom. To do that, you must understand the role of capital assets.

A capital asset is one that you build or acquire through some level of personal control. Unlike traditional investment options, capital assets are tangible assets—like businesses or real estate—over which you can exert some control and thus add to its value. You can be full owner, for example, or passive owner. You can decide how that asset is going to perform. Being involved in your capital assets can positively affect how your assets produce sustainable, predictable cash flow that you do not have to trade for your time.

Though we will fully explore capital assets in chapter 6, it's important to understand how they relate to investing in your business. The reason capital assets are so important here is because every business owner needs the ability to diversify their investments outside of their primary business in a model that has relatively low volatility, low risk, and higher predictability. Simply owning a business is not necessarily getting you closer to a Freedom Lifestyle *unless* the owner is not the primary technician of that business. If the owner prefers the technical work, then investing outside the business or practice into other capital assets is paramount.

Keep in mind that the best return on investment is derived from investing in a real business. Creating wealth and sustainable cash flow outside of the business in other capital assets should be secondary to your primary investment in your business.

As you work on building or rebuilding your business, you will endure sacrifices, but during this time, remain fixed on your goal to acquire other capital assets—plan Bs—that work for you. It's never too late or too far gone to change your life around.

Capital assets can elevate you from the overburdened role of technician wearing all the hats, spinning all the plates, to being a real business owner who has the freedom of time, energy, and passive income. With awareness and the courage to take action, you can break from the pack and find a path that leads to the Freedom Lifestyle you've imagined.

HOW SHOULD YOU INVEST IN YOUR BUSINESS?

Building a business that suits your ideal existence doesn't happen automatically. It requires much time and energy. Unless you're the benefactor of a trust fund, you'll go through a sacrifice period—a time when you have many responsibilities and must devote much of your efforts to your business.

Many people get stuck here, but those pursuing a Freedom Lifestyle recognize that once the business is established, it's time to focus on transitioning from active income—trading time for dollars—to owning a real business.

The reason you should invest in your business is because it positions you to know where the inflection points—leverage points that propel you toward freedom—are and how to use them to get you out of the sacrifice period sooner. Real freedom means you've evolved from a sacrifice period—the period of time when all your focus is on trading time for dollars, moving up Maslow's hierarchy from survival mode to safety and stability—to a lifestyle *of your choosing*.

When I talk to young professionals like Paul, I tell them that the sacrifice period is universal; the real question is how short can you make the hard sacrifice? Do you want to sacrifice your whole life, or do you want to sacrifice early and then use the Freedom Assets to catapult you closer to your true independence?

Though the sacrifice period may be a universal experience, it's not an ideal place to stay long term. So why do so many people do it? Because that's what we've been taught to do.

We've been trained to be the doer, and so we put all our efforts there. We settle for linear incremental improvements because everybody else does too. We fall prey to the trap of thinking the key to financial freedom lies in our technical skills: *If I want a better life, I need to be a more proficient and efficient technician.* This training precludes hitting an inflection point. Even more damaging is that believing the myth makes you work harder and faster, and those are not the goals.

This concept of "working hard" is wrapped up in our American culture, and I often equate this fallacy with martyrdom. Hard work is a point of pride. Maybe it's what you watched your parents and grandparents do; it's in your blood.

The reality is this is an outdated mindset that limits your potential and keeps you trapped in the sacrifice period indefinitely. There, you wait for retirement like it's an afterlife. You aren't inspired. You're aren't following your bliss. Your path feels like a predicament rather than a choice.

Another fallacy that limits your potential is believing that if you are smart and capable, then you should be able to do it all on your own. This fallacy is validated by traditional school models that often force us to work independently. This is fine during school, but once you are a business owner, this belief limits your advancement. We have to learn what collaboration looks like outside the traditional school model.

You think you should know everything and that you should be the wisest person, the most able person, the most skilled person. You believe you *are* the business. You can never leave; you can never hit any inflection points.

This is a huge burden for you to carry and ensures that you must be involved in the daily operations of the business to sustain its viability. The good news, however, is that this belief is a myth.

By releasing it as a limiting mindset, you can create new freedom opportunities for yourself and your business. By changing the dynamics of the business in small ways, you can start moving your place on the pendulum from technician to business owner.

> By changing the dynamics of the business in small ways, you can start moving your place on the pendulum from technician to business owner.

One way to invest in your business is to begin removing yourself from some of the operational business aspects. This can be done in a number of ways, but oftentimes the simplest and most efficient way to do this is to outsource some of your responsibilities.

Start by making a list of all the things that you do in a day; determine how many of these items require your full participation. Next, discern which items could be accomplished by a trusted, capable assistant who understands and shares your business goals. This list becomes the job description that you use as you hire people to assist you in the business's operational requirements.

In my own experience, one of the key people you should bring on is a personal assistant. Depending on your needs and style of business, this can be an on-site assistant or a virtual one; it can be part time or full time; it can be a professional or personal assistant— or both.

I have learned from my clients that this step can seem simple but is often quite challenging. Not because it's difficult to find proficient assistants, but because it's hard to step back and let someone else take over. For many, this is the moment you realize how enmeshed you are with your business and its responsibilities. It's akin to leaving your child with a babysitter for the first time; you want the freedom, but you also want the dependency because it offers you identity, purpose, and necessity. Sound familiar?

Another way to invest in your business is to outsource some of your technical work. Don't believe the myth that, as the technician, you're the only one skilled to do the work. I hate to be the bearer of bad news, but there are people who are as proficient as you. And they're for hire!

Keep in mind that you can train assistants. In the dental world, for example, many hygienists have impressive diagnostic skills that could benefit the main technician and elevate the business as a whole. There are also a multitude of young dental graduates who are burdened by large amounts of debt and are looking for sustainable work as an employee. They are not ready for ownership from a business management or financial standpoint, but they can alleviate some of your technical work.

It's easy to limit yourself by saying, "Well, I can just do it faster. I don't have time to explain things to someone else." This is a hurdle between yourself and freedom. To clear it, make sure that you make good hiring decisions.

Don't look for an assistant or a technician who merely takes orders. Find someone who has the capability to look at outcomes with you, who can consider net results, who helps you accomplish your goals. Also remember that every position for which you hire should be self-funding—meaning that person is paying for themselves because what they do adds multiples over what they're being paid. Don't be afraid to pay for superior talent, to compensate well. One highly proficient team member can often outperform two or three other average members.

A lot of business owners think they need to improve their revenue first. They spend time and energy chasing more customers, clients, or patients, when in fact, these same businesses would benefit from first improving their current inefficiencies.

When you look closer at the business processes, you often find that most small businesses don't build trusting relationships to maximize the potential value of the patient services they provide. Maybe before you sink more time and energy into chasing new customers, there needs to be a redesign of the business. Maybe you need to reconsider how you retain your client base. For example, what is the patient or customer experience like from the phone intake to the continued care? Rather than spending resources adding to the business, oftentimes the best strategy is enriching the quality of the current business.

KEYS TO OPTIMIZING YOUR PRACTICE:

1. Have a strong team culture and competent leadership other than yourself.

2. Have accurate and reliable financial forecasts for next

month, next quarter, and next year.

3.   Have a strong marketing message that is consistently attracting quality new customers.

4.   Have well-documented systems and processes throughout the organization.

5.   Be able to step away from your business for thirty days or more without affecting production.

Of course it takes time and energy to invest in a business. Until you have weathered the sacrifice period and have created some space to view your business objectively, it can be difficult to identify your blind spots. I admit, being objective as the business owner is difficult. It's the concept of not being able to see the forest because one is down working among all the trees.

When we don't have time and energy, we don't dig in, and then we don't find out. Having help can free up a lot of brain space. It allows you to focus your energy *on* your business instead of *in* your business.

LESSONS LEARNED

After I had been an associate dentist for several years, I started thinking about owning my own practice. Like Dr. Paul, I saw my colleagues taking this route and believed this was the inevitable next step. The first step was finding a location.

Because of my real estate investment experience, I decided I'd rather own a building than lease one. This was in the early 1990s after the savings and loan debacle, so many properties in the South were being auctioned off. I ended up getting a building fairly inexpensively and then underwent the process of designing and executing a build-out.

At that time, marketing involved getting your name in the phone book and then on the building, so that's what I did. I hired three people—two assistants and a hygienist. Then I did what all my peers did—I hit the ground running.

I did find joy in my practice and my patients, but the grunt work quickly began to take its toll. I often spent large portions of my days doing administrative tasks. I had constant backaches from the work. Once my daughter was born, I resented the time I "had" to spend at the office. I wanted to be a good provider for my family, but I often wondered what I was giving up in pursuit of this.

I still continued my real estate investments on the side, which also brought me joy. I had an entire network of real estate contacts and friends whom I met with regularly. At this point, my life was segmented: I was a dentist by day and a real estate investor by night.

Once Jenna started having health problems, the pressure on me increased. I felt my family needed my income more than ever, but they also needed *me* more than ever. It wasn't until I was in the hospital with my daughter that I had the literal time and space from my practice to see how it was trapping me.

Once I had the awareness that my business was running me, I decided to take action. Because I had been doing real estate for over a decade at this point, I knew I had some passive income, but was it enough?

I realized that, even though I'm a planner by nature, I had never taken stock of my assets. I had built up a certain amount of real estate assets outside of my technical work at this point, but I had never taken the measurement of them because I didn't need to.

In what would become the model that I now share with clients,

I devised my Freedom Number—how much passive income I would need to replace the active income made from being a dentist. To my surprise, my passive cash flow slightly exceeded what I needed to assure a secure lifestyle maintenance for my family. The passive income number wasn't huge. It didn't replace what I could produce working full time in my dental practice. However, when I considered how much we needed to live and not suffer financially, it was enough. That was the key. I had reached my minimum viable Freedom Number, and I had the assurance that I could financially leave my practice. Now I just had to figure out how to expediently sell the practice.

In 2005, after twenty-two years in practice, I put my business on the market. Not long after, I had an interested buyer, and because I was motivated, I took more risks than I should have. I agreed to finance the seller. If the story ended there, it would seem like a straight, easy journey toward financial freedom. That was not the case, however.

I sold to a capable, but flawed, younger dentist. Being a determined seller, I agreed to carry the note—called seller financing—until he could improve his credit and refinance me out. That never happened. First lesson learned.

I had to take back the practice in 2007 through a long, expensive, and messy litigation process. When I regained my practice, it was in shambles. The best patients were gone as well as half the original staff. The usual course of action? Suit back up and do what I had been trained to do: dentistry. But now things were different. Jenna was recovering from a liver transplant. She'd survived leukemia, epilepsy, and multiple treatments and surgeries. She needed me. Was I really going to let myself be trapped again? Absolutely not.

So what could I do about it? I decided to bring the practice back to profitability and resell it without being the primary producer (dentist). I had to become a real business owner, not a technician. Easy? No. Doable? Yes, with commitment.

For more than twenty years, I had focused on improving my dental skills, learning new procedures, and working more efficiently at a higher dollar per hour. I was a technician. This time, however, I wanted to be a real business owner; I focused on marketing, leadership, and communication, along with operational (deliverables) excellence and sales process and conversion. I relied on my professional network for consulting and advice to give me the inflection point I needed. Moreover, I did it through *other* people's time, talent, and skills—not mine. Another lesson learned.

I recruited three associate doctors who all had the opportunity to buy the practice as long as they could do it with bank financing— no more carrying the note for me. We expanded hours and became consumer driven. The best part for me, however, was that I was no longer involved in the operations. I was a real owner of a real business!

In 2010, three years after my first failed attempt to sell my practice, I was able to sell to one of the associate doctors—with 100 percent bank financing and during the depth of the Great Recession, no less. This was a revelation of what I always thought was possible— you can run a business without it running you. Because I had never pushed myself to see if it could work, I never knew. Now I knew, and I wouldn't stop sharing the message with others.

■ ■ ■

I have been both a technician and a real business owner; I have owned both a failing business and a productive one. No matter the current state of your asset, you can turn it around. Don't fall prey to the myth that you must make your business bigger to be successful. The idea that we have to expand, add more locations, and be a multiple owner does not expediate our path to freedom. In fact, it often distances us from it.

Start where you are with what you have. As Arthur Ashe, famous tennis star of the 1980s, once said, "Start where you are. Use what you have. Do what you can." No matter the current state of the business, or your role in it, there are always opportunities present.

If you own a business that requires your presence every day, that's bleeding you dry, that's failing—you still have the chance to turn it around. In fact, if this is your situation, you have an even stronger reason *why*.

As I shared with Dr. Paul when he first came to me, though I can provide the model for transitioning from technician to business owner, I can't provide the *why*. As long as you have that, you have the tools you need to invest in your business.

Once you have the business working well as a real business, then you can start creating wealth and other passive income streams outside the business in the alternative space of real estate. That's how you progress on your own Freedom Curve—the pathway to achieve true freedom sooner in life than the traditional path; you put your business first, and then you start moving into the outside wealth categories. Over time, you'll be doing what you want to do, when you want to do it, with whom you want to do it, and where you want to do it.

TAKEAWAYS :

- A real business is a capital asset that can grow wealth and achieve freedom if done wisely.

- Once you have the awareness about whether your role is that of technician or business owner, that's the turning point, the opportunity to take action and become one step closer to a Freedom Lifestyle.

- The best return on investment is derived from investing in a real business. Creating wealth and sustainable cash flow outside the business in other capital assets should be secondary to your primary investment in your business.

- You will endure a sacrifice period—a time when you have many responsibilities and must devote much of your efforts to your business—but during this time, remain fixed on your goal to acquire other capital assets that work for you.

- The reason you should invest in your business is because it positions you to know where the inflection points are— leverage points that propel you toward freedom—and how to use them to get you out of the sacrifice period sooner.

- To invest in your business, begin removing yourself from some of the operational business aspects, outsource some of your responsibilities, and optimize your existing practice.

CHAPTER 5

Invest in Your Relationships

I'll never forget my first meeting with Freedom Founders. It was mind blowing—like drinking from a fire hose. It's so refreshing to be in a room with like-minded people who give you advice and sincerely want you to benefit. I have built valuable relationships with Trusted Advisors and others in the room. I know that I'm in good hands.

—Dr. Raj Dhamrait

■ ■ ■

When discussing financial freedom, many conversations center on capital—building capital, investing capital, trading capital. Unfortunately, we spend little time talking about the most valuable aspect of all—human capital.

Relationships create your environment, your reality, your network. When people think about networks, they often think about networking—going to conferences, passing out business cards, staying connected on LinkedIn. Considering that your network is your net worth, it's time to transition from networking to building a network that can be a powerful asset on your path toward freedom.

Speaker and author Jim Rohn is well known for claiming, "You are the average of the five people you spend the most time with." His idea borrows from the law of averages—that the result of any given situation will be the average of all outcomes. For this reason, you need to be as intentional about investing in your relationships as you are about investing in other assets. According to the law of averages, by choosing your network wisely—your top five—you are increasing the likelihood of your own success.

I like to view networks as rings of influence, with you in the center. The concentric rings around you represent your relationships. The first ring would be your family and closest friends; the second ring should be your top five, as Rohn puts it. Rings three and four are your respective personal and professional relationships. The outer ring represents the more tertiary relationships, like online friends.

These five rings of influence might vary in emotional importance, but it's the second ring that we will primarily focus on in this chapter, because it can expediate and validate your path toward freedom.

RINGS OF INFLUENCE

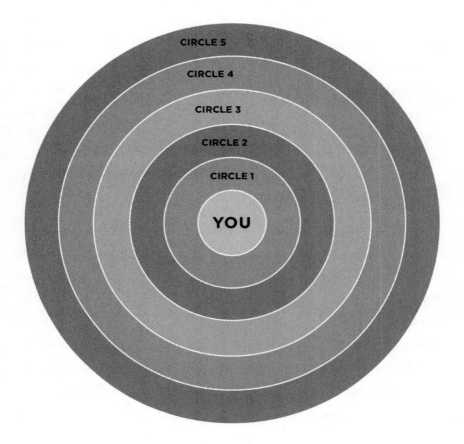

By choosing your networks—or rings of influence—wisely, you are increasing the likelihood of your own successful outcomes.

At Freedom Founders, we often ask one another, "Do you have your top five?" Keeping in mind that your five will organically evolve as you do, it's still important to put some thought into your networks. I often tell my clients that a great way to practice this is to make sure you are not the smartest person in the room. Instead, find groups that challenge you.

What often happens in Freedom Founders is that people join

our community and then organically find their five. These smaller networks become quite meaningful and powerful for their members. For example, a group of five doctors who came from different backgrounds and lifestyles quickly forged a bond through their connection at Freedom Founders workshop. Initially, much of their communication was about professional and investment matters. Over the course of a year, however, their dynamic shifted to something deeper. They now have weekly calls together to check in about life, work, investments, and anything else they are experiencing.

Witnessing their friendship and respective successes are good reminders that having a supportive, challenging network around you can elevate your accomplishments and expedite your achievements. These are human relationships built on trust, accountability, and respect. Furthermore, the members challenge each other. This is perhaps one of the greatest benefits of having the right network. Being surrounded by people who test you, your beliefs, and your limitations can be the difference between mediocrity and dynamism.

Recently this same group met up for an underwriting trip with a Freedom Founders Trusted Advisor to discuss a real estate deal. They were like a small tribe reviewing the deal, questioning the deal, negotiating the deal. Whereas many entrepreneurs are solopreneurs, making decisions based on their own limited training and fields, these five were working together, sharing their skills, and multiplying their strengths. With the added advantage of four other opinions, their decisions and strategies were well planned, well researched, and well executed.

From my experience, a lot of hardworking solopreneurs feel like they're all alone, in part because collaboration is rarely taught in traditional education, as we've discussed. Many of us were taught that everything we did in life was going to be about us. Instead of emphasizing teamwork, the focus was on exams, tests, boards, your own individual potential. You did things on your own because you had to prove yourself, which created generations of adults who feel burdened by the need to do it all alone.

This is a self-limiting belief that leads to more burnout, more exhaustion, and more stagnancy. With this traditional approach to networking, there's never a next. There is no support, validation, or encouragement to help forge a plan. When there is no next, that's the end. You're done.

For most solopreneurs who've developed an individualist-style approach due to necessity, learning to collaborate is challenging. Teaching people how to collaborate and form strategic alliances is a key part of leveraging yourself to that next wealth level of the Freedom Curve. On the path to freedom, you'll need to understand how to collaborate, how to lead and delegate, how to hire exceptional staff, and how to surround yourself with challenging people. You're orchestrating, but you're doing it through other people, not by yourself.

> Teaching people how to collaborate and form strategic alliances is a key part of leveraging yourself to that next wealth level of the Freedom Curve.

For those who have veered from the traditional path of work and wealth building, the journey can be lonely. Suddenly finding a tribe of other renegade entrepreneurs can be a profoundly validating experience. You no longer spend your mental energy (and time) questioning your decisions or comparing your alternative approach to the traditional approach. You have a group that can support your mindset, challenge you on your alternate path to wealth building, and support your singular focus of achieving a Freedom Lifestyle.

HOW SHOULD YOU INVEST IN RELATIONSHIPS?

If you want to change your life, you must start with the way you think about yourself. You can change the way you think about your life and yourself only if you change the people with whom you spend the most time. You have to choose your network carefully. It doesn't mean you disavow other friends and social contexts, but you have to be discerning about who feeds your mind if you're going to rise up and become a better person.

Many people are familiar with the concept of strategic alliances as they relate to businesses—meaning two independent companies find places where they can collaborate and synergize without requiring a full business juncture, or partnership. The same can be said of personal strategic alliances.

So often we focus on our weaknesses, but with a network of personal strategic alliances filling in those deficiencies, the focus is on your strengths. That's true collaboration and allows you to focus on what you do well—your unique abilities. The world moves too fast with too much information, for one person to try to master it all. Don't try to do everything; don't try to be a generalist. Just figure out what you do well, what you like to do, and then fill in the gaps with other people.

There are many examples of this type of collaboration, perhaps the best being Apple's Steve Jobs and Steve Wozniak. Jobs was the visionary whose aptitude was carrying and communicating a vision. It was Wozniak who was the technician. Jobs probably couldn't even begin to do what Wozniak did, but he didn't need to. He surrounded himself with personal strategic alliances, and that's in part what drove Apple's success.

There are several reasons why investing in your relationships can benefit you personally and professionally. If any one business or enterprise is so dependent on one person—typically the solopreneur—and that person needs to be out for a period of time, what happens to that business? It suffers. You don't want a business that is primarily dependent on one person. For your own sake, you need to have some redundancy through other people.

On the offensive side, you need collaboration to enrich your products and services. My inner leadership team—called Advocates— for example, is composed of four other individuals. Because we each have different strengths, we make it a point to discuss the undiscussable. Nothing is off the table. I often remind them, "I have a vision, but I also have a bias. Your job as my strategic network is to challenge my vision with your own ideas. Be convicted about them. Just bring it." I don't want a team that is submissive and eternally agreeable. I want a team that steps up and challenges me because that makes all of us stronger.

It makes you more dynamic to be around collaborators who will identify your blind spots and challenge your thinking. It's like having an informal board of advisers. When these alliances are formed, trust is built, and synergy is achieved. This creates more opportunities to do business.

Freedom Founders, for example, collaborates with other people and their businesses because there are complementary aspects we can offer each other. I speak at other people's events because I bring something they lack; likewise, I often have my collaborators speak at my events because they bring resources I don't specialize in. This collaboration is a big leverage or inflection point when it comes to fostering personal and professional success.

Businessman and best-selling author Harvey Mackay once wrote, "If I had to name the single characteristic shared by all the truly successful people I've met over a lifetime, I'd say it is the ability to create and nurture a network of contacts."[7] Known for his infamous Rolodex that held more than six thousand contacts, he also said, "Our lives basically change in two ways—the people we meet and the books we read.

"Trust me—the people you meet every day are extremely important in building your network. In my entire career I have never once heard a successful person say they regretted putting time and energy into keeping their Rolodex file."[8] Okay, so his metaphor might now be outdated, but you get the message.

It's true that you never know who could be in your five, or in any of those circles of influence. For that reason, you want to be open to strategic alliances. At the same time, you want to maintain filters to determine who to invite into those inner circles. If you let too many people in, or the wrong people in, it can have a negative effect.

Oftentimes my clients are confounded by how and where to find their networks. The best answer I can offer is to share my own experience doing so. In my early twenties, when I was investing in myself through self-education, I went to my first real estate seminar hosted by a man who would became one of the key mentors in my life: Jack Miller.

Jack had an acumen for business, real estate, and finance, but he also had a sharp mind about people and human behavior. I remember at that first seminar, he posed the question, "If you had to leave the country for six months, how many people in your life would you trust to manage your bank accounts, assets, and personal responsibilities?"

---

7 Harvey Mackay, *Use Your Head to Get Your Foot in the Door: Job Search Secrets No One Else Will Tell You* (New York: Penguin, 2010).

8 Harvey Mackay, "Dig Your Well before You're Thirsty," *Harvey Mackay* (blog), January 11, 2018, https://harveymackay.com/dig-well-youre-thirsty/.

I scanned the room, but no one raised their hand. I didn't put it all together at the time, but Jack's question stayed with me, and I made some long-term friendships during those seminars. Outside of the emotional reward, building a network outside my industry would soon serve me well—and continue to do so for the next forty years.

Stepping outside the dental industry to build my network validated my thinking. Rather than work within the confines of my own training and industry, I put myself in front of people who challenged my instincts and my traditional path. When you're open, those connections start appearing. Jack eventually led me to another mentor who led me to another mentor, and the cycle continued. Suddenly I was given permission to think differently, to be who I *was* without society dictating who I *should be*.

Without an outside network, you adopt the thinking of the people who trained like you, worked like you, saved like you, are trapped like you. A lot of people have a sunk cost fallacy that controls their decision-making and long-term planning: *I put all my time and money into my education. There's no way I can leave it. People will think I'm crazy if I switch careers or make a drastic change.*

When I was considering selling my practice, if I had spoken with other dentists who

> A lot of people have a sunk cost fallacy that controls their decision-making and long-term planning.

had been in practice for over twenty years like myself, they would have said I was foolish to abandon what I'd built. They would say that I had no choice but to stay the course. Being around a real estate network, however, allowed me to think outside of my specialized training.

I could see that many people left their careers in pursuit of capital assets through real estate. I wasn't unwise; I was questioning. My network challenged my thinking and gave me permission to make the bold move in pursuit of my next. These relationships proved to be an invaluable part of my path to freedom and were the impetus for creating the Freedom Founders Mastermind Group—to create a network of thought leaders from whom to get advice.

If you'd like to join the dozens of dentists, docs, and practice professionals on the fast track to freedom (three to five years), visit FreedomFounders.com/Step-1 to apply for a guest seat.

I will admit that though I appreciate the power of relationships, establishing them does not come easily to me. I'm not the most socially adept person. I'm not a social magnet. In fact, people wear me out—not *all* people—just people in general. I like people, but large groups, masses, and big get-togethers of any kind drain energy from me.

I'm most at home in small groups or one to one. When I'm in a room where I don't know anybody, I'm quiet. I have to force myself to be the person who makes connections easily. I push myself out of my comfort zone.

While I'll never be the life of the party or walk into a *Cheers* bar and have everybody know my name, I'm comfortable with who I am. Well, most of the time.

When I'm in meetings, for example, I actively listen to what people are sharing and assess any commonalities that exist. I might then seek that person out at a break and say, "I enjoyed your contribution." Maybe I'll point out something we have in common—an experience, a colleague, a value. Oftentimes this connection is something personal, not professional.

When you connect with someone on a personal basis, you're showing that you have an interest in them as a person, not just in their business acumen or achievements. If I continue to feel a connection, then I work to further build rapport. Maybe I send a quick note after the conference or set up a phone call. Maybe we make plans for coffee or a quick meetup before the next meeting.

Keep in mind that strategic relationships need not be reciprocal. If I meet someone I feel a connection with, and I understand who they are and what they need, I seek ways to help them. With a service-oriented attitude, I can perhaps connect them with other people who might specialize in a skill they require. Serving first without any expectations of returns is the way to build enriching relationships.

After you have built your network, the work doesn't stop there. You must continue to cultivate these relationships. There are many ways to do this. Easy ways to cultivate the connections you make are through handwritten cards and letters, virtual cards, or newsletters. Personalized videos are also easy to make and rewarding to receive.

For me, I write a monthly newsletter that I send to my influencer list—people in my space with whom I intentionally build relationships. Even though this is a one-way conversation, it keeps the connection present. When I run into members of this network at conferences, for example, there is a familiarity established. From their standpoint, our relationship feels tighter because they know what I have been doing. If I one day needed their help, they would be more apt to take my call, even if we haven't talked for two years, because I have done something in the meantime to nurture the relationship.

KEYS TO BUILDING AND CULTIVATING YOUR NETWORK:

- When you meet with your peers, try to make sure you are not the smartest person in the room.

- Have a board of advisers that you use to solve your top business challenges.

- Have peers who know your goals and who have permission to help you address blind spots.

- Try to find your tribe of like-minded peers.

- Try to gain access to positive role models who have achieved what you are seeking in your own life.

Having people around you who give you permission to question the status quo is extremely important. You need others who can empower your mindset. When society tells you no, you need people to embolden you to ask, *Why not?* Too many people give up when they hit resistance and continue to live by society's agenda. This traps people into one career, one financial bracket, one life.

What I know now is that the majority of the world does live in a "work mentality." Our schools create this mindset. Go to school, work hard, get good grades and scholarships, and go as high on the education ladder as possible so that you can enter a great career. That's the formula for a successful life (so they say).

That's false. A myth. A lie. The time-for-dollars model is a trap! It's a strictly linear model with no leverage. I'd still be there if not for the wisdom and insights that I gleaned from mentors early in my life and to whom I am ever so grateful today. These mentors gave me a life perspective that I had never heard—not from my awesome and hardworking parents, not from any of my grade school teachers, community leaders, college professors, graduate school advisers, and teachers.

As good as they were at what they did, they did not have a good view of the world. They couldn't teach me how to leverage my personal strengths and assets to have, not just a successful life, but an incredible, purposeful, and influential life.

My passion in life far exceeds the success definitions of society, based primarily on income and materialism. Is money important? Of course. We exchange money for what we want more of in life, whatever that is. For me, the exchange is time and influence. I use money to buy time and influence through collaboration with other people, joint ventures and strategic alliances, employees, and vendors. It wasn't a luxury that I had when I was young and had more time than money.

Crossing the transition line to leveraging everything you can in life is critical, but few make that transition and instead get stuck on a hamster wheel. To build and leverage a network—relationship capital—I had to step it up. Yep, even as an introvert, I knew that people—the right people—were the key to a meaningful future.

I'll never be a natural "front stage guy." But I know I am capable of pushing myself to do it. I have a strong reason *why*. I know that if I am going to have more influence, serve more people, and remain the visionary and leader of my tribe, I have to continually push myself to be more. It's my cause and mission to be a transforming leader for those who also want to live differently. It's a personal challenge.

You can't do this alone. Find your tribe. Find your people who understand you and like you and are in pursuit of an uncommon life. Find your *Cheers* bar. They're out there. It's up to you to become uncomfortable enough to seek them out.

Investing in networks like Freedom Founders, where you have mentorship, community, and accountability, pays dividends. With a trusted network in place, you will make fewer mistakes. Every time I've made a decision of any substance on my own, there have been things I overlooked and wished I'd done differently. When I can check in with my trusted advisers, however, they can help me see those potential pitfalls before I make the decision. This has spared me much time, effort, and money fixing mistakes.

Furthermore, when I can collaborate with others and have the benefit of their strengths, then the implementation of my ideas is better. If I can focus on what I do best as a visionary without fracturing my time and energy trying to also be the implementer, then I can build greater things. Without a network, you can only go so far, and there's no leverage to it. There's an inherent ceiling on everything you try to accomplish yourself.

Transforming requires a change in your environment. Changing your beliefs requires changing your circles of influence, your people, your tribe. This isn't a moral judgment of the people with whom you currently associate. It would help if you had a community of individuals who are on a similar path—people with whom you can relate, people you can trust, people who don't have an agenda, and people who believe that true collaboration is the height of freedom.

INVEST IN YOUR FAMILY

Too often we get caught up in our professional networks and forget the whole reason we needed a network in the first place—to free up time in the Five Freedoms to invest in those relationships represented by the first circle in the rings of influence. Professional networks empower your unique abilities so that you have time to invest back in your family, which is what we all inherently seek.

I saw it in my own life when my daughter was young, and I see it over and over in my clients' lives—we spend our time and efforts building businesses to have an influence on the world; meanwhile, our own families are waiting patiently for their turn with our time

104 FindYourNext.com

and attention. This is the top regret that many of my clients face in their later years. And they're not alone.

As a palliative care nurse in Australia, Bronnie Ware spent much of her time talking with her dying patients about regret. Over time, she noticed a pattern in the sorrows people held at the end of their lives. In her best-selling memoir, *The Top Five Regrets of the Dying*, she offers the recurring laments her dying patients shared with her in their final days:[9]

1. I wish I'd had the courage to live a life true to myself, not the life others expected of me.

2. I wish I hadn't worked so hard.

3. I wish I'd had the courage to express my feelings.

4. I wish I had stayed in touch with my friends.

5. I wish that I had let myself be happier.

What is most interesting about Ware's conversations is the omission of achievements. Of the second regret about having worked too hard, Ware shares, "This came from every male patient that I nursed. They missed their children's youth and their partner's companionship. Women also spoke of this regret. But as most were from an older generation, many of the female patients had not been breadwinners. All of the men I nursed deeply regretted spending so much of their lives on the treadmill of a work existence."[10]

At the end of their lives, her patients weren't ruminating on their careers or how much success they enjoyed; instead, their focus had shifted to the reward of time spent with their families and loved ones. This list of regrets is perhaps the greatest motivator for a Freedom

9   Bronnie Ware, *The Top Five Regrets of the Dying* (London: Hay House, 2012).

10 Bronnie Ware, "Regrets of the Dying," *Bronnie Ware* (blog), https://bronnieware.com/blog/regrets-of-the-dying/.

Lifestyle. Sure, financial freedom feels great, but it is certainly not the sweetest reward.

WANT TO WORK WITH ME DIRECTLY?

If you'd like to work directly with me and a small group of my closest investment colleagues, with direct access to the dealmakers and asset classes that I invest in, just send a message to admin@freedomfounders.com and put "Fast Access" in the subject line. Or call (972) 203-6960 (ext. 160) and leave a brief voice mail. Let us know if you're interested in the Fast Access program—we'll set up a time with you to talk, find out about your goals, and see if there is a fit.

When I talk with clients, I accept where they are today. I know what their priorities are because I know what mine were at that stage of life—they're worried about money, responsibilities, and achievement. Another benefit of a varied network is that you can escape the bubble created by your age, naiveté, or inexperience and pace yourself to see what will be important to you in ten, twenty, forty years.

Doing so allows you to appreciate the gifts in front of you rather than focusing on the achievements behind you. This is perhaps one of the greatest values of a network. Never forget that the greatest by-product of all your efforts to achieve a Freedom Lifestyle is more time with the people and things you love. Perhaps the greatest freedom is a life lived with no regrets.

TAKEAWAYS :

- Be as intentional about investing in your relationships as you are about investing in other assets. According to the law of averages, by choosing your networks wisely, you are increasing the likelihood of your own successful outcomes.

- If you want to change your life, you must start with the way you think about yourself. You can transform the way you think about your life and yourself only if you alter the environment of people with whom you spend the most time.

- After you have built your network, the work doesn't stop there. You must continue to cultivate these relationships.

- Without a network, you can go only so far, and there's no leverage to it. There's an inherent ceiling on everything you try to accomplish yourself.

- Professional networks empower your unique abilities so that you have time to invest back in your family, which is what we all inherently seek.

CHAPTER 6

Invest in Your Capital

Making more money and becoming more profitable in practice is the first step. To create real freedom the way Dr. David Phelps teaches means keeping more of the money one earns and then putting that money to work to eventually replace our labor-produced income. I am a huge believer in passive income streams and David's Freedom Blueprint program.

—Dr. Brady Frank

■ ■ ■

After my daughter's arduous postoperative recovery at Texas Children's Hospital, she was in and out of the hospital due to a series of complications. At one point, she had a constriction in her bile duct, so she was scheduled for yet another corrective follow-up surgery. It was during her recovery from this surgery that I sat on a vinyl bench in her room silently watching her sleep.

After months of going back and forth from her bedside to my dental practice, I was quiet, still, and focused on the small triumphs of her breaths. A breath in. *Thank God.* A breath out. *Thank God.*

On the shelf behind her hospital bed, I counted twenty bottles of medication helping to keep my daughter's young body functioning properly. How many breaths had I taken for granted? How many times had I rushed from one detail to the next, never appreciating the new day I'd been gifted?

Staring at the arsenal of medications behind her, I was struck by the reality of her life—she would be dependent on medications for immunosuppression for life. Her breaths would not always come easy. She would have an appreciation for life that I had yet to understand.

We expect older people to lead full lives that run their courses, but staring at my twelve-year-old fighting harder than many people will ever have to, I felt ashamed at how many hours, days, years I'd taken for granted. I had never been a pessimist, but suddenly I was a devout realist, and it was time to get real about the preciousness of life. I knew logically that each day was a blessing, but for the most part, I had taken life—and family—for granted. Each day was a gift I had not respected up to this point.

For decades, I had spent all my time on my career, my family, and my investments. Every day was a new list of things to do. I was rarely idle with time to ponder. Sitting on that bench in the hospital, there was nothing to do but think.

This was the first time in a long time that the outside world was kept away from me. No one needed me. There were no responsibilities vying for my attention. The only thing that mattered was what was literally laid out in front of me—my daughter and her small precious breaths.

With the empty time I had sitting by Jenna's bed, I pondered my life and how I might make a drastic change. How could I stop being chained to a job, albeit a respectable one, with a relatively high dollar exchange for my time? Where was I in my life? Where did I ideally want to be?

I understood that point A was where I was that day; point B was where I wanted to be. In between those two points was the gap, and within the gap was the barrier that needed to be identified. Only then could I explore possible solutions.

While my chosen training and career in dentistry provided me the means to create relatively strong, sustainable income by trading my time, that exchange was keeping my choices limited. I decided that a life with limited choices was not a good life. I needed the freedom of options.

How could I achieve that when I was scheduled out more than six months in advance? I was at war with myself in those moments. The technician in me said, *David, if you don't get up and go to work on this schedule, then you're not doing what you spent your life training and earning the right to do.* But the father and entrepreneur in me countered, *David, how much is your training worth when it limits your financial freedom, time freedom, relationship freedom, health freedom, and purpose freedom?*

What followed in the days after these realizations about the preciousness of life was more "think time" to ask myself challenging questions and provide myself authentic answers that might help me find a path toward a life that afforded me more freedom of finances, time, relationships, and health.

What are the reasons I'm experiencing this situation? I had built a business around doing the thing, dentistry, which meant if I didn't show up on a regular schedule, the business didn't work. This is what society told me was the way to build a life, but at what cost?

What wasn't happening that, if it did happen, would narrow the gap or cause these symptoms in the gap to disappear? Could other people do the thing, dentistry, that I had been primarily responsible for doing?

What is happening that, if it happened more, would narrow the gap or cause these symptoms to disappear? For me, it was being out of the office. What if everybody else stepped up? Maybe the associate would step up and cover for me? Maybe the patients would step up and agree to see the associate? Maybe the staff would step up and communicate with patients, validate the associate, and offer solutions?

I had to ask myself more difficult questions that I had never asked before: *How much money is enough to provide my freedom? Do I have enough passive income to provide what I need?* I wasn't sure how to answer this, but I knew the answer to this question could change my future and my family's future.

Up until that point, I had never answered these questions because, like most people, I just was going to keep doing what I was doing. Looking at my daughter fighting for her life (again) in a hospital bed made me critically aware of my traditional mindset and the ways it was limiting my happiness and potential.

What I would soon realize was that I did have enough passive income to provide what I needed. With several more months of intentional decision-making and decisive action, I could have the freedom and choices I had been seeking.

Without think time in the hospital, sharing a room with the most valuable person to me, I wouldn't have achieved the clarity of thought to determine what would years later become my freedom-based approach to work and wealth and provide the foundation for a Freedom Lifestyle.

WHY DO YOU INVEST IN CAPITAL?

Freedom is about having choices and options. Restricted choices lead to restricted lives. We often limit our choices by following the majority, allowing society to define our success. This thinking affects our behavior and leads us into the traditional ball-and-chain lifestyle. Though the traditional path offers the hope of working hard all your life and then enjoying the fruits of your labor, it's not a realistic process, in part because of the misuse of capital assets.

For most people, once you get into a career, it's a linear advancement. You make enough for your short-term needs, while your long-term plan is to work until you're in your sixties and can retire. You may make a little money and even have a nice house, but you don't have freedom of time, money, or purpose.

Initially, capital is money that we work for by trading time for dollars. When we have money, then we have some choices. Perhaps the most important choice is deciding what to do with the money you earn. Typically, you spend money on the basic necessities—shelter, clothing, transportation, utilities. Other times, you might spend that money on things you want or to pay off debt.

In chapter 4, I acknowledged that the sacrifice period—a period of time when you are building active income by trading time for dollars—is universal. This is not time wasted, however. As I discovered while I sat in my daughter's hospital room, having time to think and strategize about your short-term needs and your long-term goals can have a profound effect on how long you stay in this period.

This is the time to discern your Freedom Number—the monthly passive income amount required to replace your active trading time for dollars income. It's easier for most people to come up with a monthly amount they require—their monthly burn rate—because it's more tangible. We multiply it by twelve to get an annual amount and then gross it up for taxes. Having this number goal in mind makes your sacrifice period shorter, more tolerable, and more productive.

Furthermore, when you have your Freedom Number, the sacrifice becomes more conscious, and it is easier to do without certain things. As mentioned, many people fall prey to the trap of affluence. To feel successful or worthy, we think we need big houses, fancy cars, and extravagant trips.

When you view such expenditures in the context of your time, you will not fall prey to their trappings. Instead, you will compare the purchase of a new car, for example, with the time it will take you to make up for the purchase. That will certainly put things in perspective! You can have the car, but then you might have to add another year or two to your sacrifice period. Is it worth it? Only you can answer.

When my daughter was in the hospital struggling for her life, extravagances became tertiary. I realized that if I could get my Freedom Number low enough, I could actually transition out of my sacrifice period into my Freedom Lifestyle. I was forced to stop, think, and acknowledge the harsh reality that time with my daughter might be limited. Nothing else mattered but getting my number low enough to have more time with her.

Once you have your Freedom Number in mind, your sacrifice period shortens from several decades to under a decade, depending on your existing debt and Freedom Number. For Freedom Founders members, we are able to get them to their goal in three to five years.

Imagine what this understanding and goal setting does to your outlook. When you start a career, you know you have this unseen goal of retirement. Even though you can't see it, you know (hope!) it's there. But when you're within vision of it, even if you're tired and worn out, you get that burst of energy. Now you can do it!

Instead of this abstract retirement in your sixties, you now have a quantifiable goal, a finish line within view. Now you can envision what that life looks like, which gives you a lot of joy and motivation to continue on.

Once you determine your Freedom Number, how do you shorten your sacrifice period? You stay focused on recognizing and using inflection points. As we've discussed, inflection points are leverage points that provide large gains, and they exist in your personal, business, and investment spheres.

When you hit an inflection point, you have the potential to go from linear advancement to exponential advancement. The problem is that most people overlook inflection points because they follow the majority, who also overlooks them. (I learned many years ago not to follow the majority because the majority is usually wrong.) Because of the power that inflection points hold, one of the key areas Kandace and I focus on with Freedom Founders members during their Freedom Blueprint Days at our home in Texas is the specific inflection points relevant to the client.

As we discussed in chapter 4, as you transition out of your sacrifice period, there's an inflection point where your wealth starts to work for you. With this bump, you're able to begin transitioning away from trading time for dollars. You're able to focus on creating freedom in all aspects of your life.

When you hit your Freedom Number, all the other freedoms will expand because you basically have bought yourself time. It's much easier to sacrifice when you are working toward the goal of the Five Freedoms—purpose, health, relationships, time, and finance.

A NOTE ON INVESTING IN YOUR HEALTH:

It may be atypical to think of health as a capital asset to invest in, but that's exactly why I made it one of the Freedom Assets. It's overlooked too often, but it is the cornerstone of a Freedom Lifestyle. If you have compromised health, then you have limited some choices. If you can't travel, for example, you have restricted options.

The whole premise of freedom is providing yourself expanded choices. If you're limiting your health assets, then you have reduced some of your freedom.

When my daughter was ill and I was shouldering the burden of being a technician trading time for dollars, I was not well. I had to give up something, and unfortunately, I gave up my health.

Countless times I have counseled clients who worked hard their whole lives, inching toward their finish line of retirement. When they get there, they realize they might not be financially sound enough to retire or not well enough to enjoy their golden years.

My own mom and dad are examples of this. My parents worked hard and were able to retire in their early sixties. They were actively traveling and enjoying life when my mother died suddenly from a pulmonary embolism when she was seventy. I learned then that you can't wait and assume you will have a full life ahead of you. You must be proactive and intentional about your health. If you're not, then what's the point of freedom?

This is certainly not a health manual. We all know the

tenets of a healthy life—move your body and nourish it well. Though there are myriad diseases, the root of all illness and disease is inflammation. What is a major cause of inflammation? Stress.

When you limit your stressors, you limit your inflammation and thereby your propensity for illness. How stressed are you? How inflamed are you? In giving yourself more choices, you're in essence limiting your inflammation levels. On a cellular level, everything's functioning as it should be.

You can't control all aspects of your health, but you can control the things that weigh you down. In freeing yourself of those, you are embracing a future filled with health, happiness, and freedom. To your health!

HOW CAN YOU INVEST IN CAPITAL?

Too many people focus on the short game—today's stressors, today's obligations, today's bills. These are short-term worries and not the long game. When you consider your future and the choices you hope to have available to you, then you are motivated by the long game.

Both perspectives are important, but most people ignore the long game and in turn miss capital investment opportunities. A wise investment creates more choices, which equals greater freedom.

We all want more money because we all want more freedom, more choices. This is where capital becomes an integral part of the Freedom approach. Without appropriate capital assets and cash flow generation, we get trapped on the traditional path of trading time for dollars and struggling to crawl over the finish line of retirement.

When it comes to money, you want to make wise, informed, deliberate choices so that you can build more money and create future options and choices for yourself. If you fail to invest at all, or if you fail to invest wisely, then you limit your future choices. For this reason, you need to put money toward capital investments.

Once you have capital, it's important that you invest it in ways that make your dollars work as hard as you worked for them. Traditionally, people hold assets in the financial market, including Wall Street funds, stocks, bonds, and annuities. This is typical and easy, but there are many issues with this asset management.

The volatility of these markets makes them bad stewards of people's money. Rarely do people feel confident about such investments, and as too many people know, they can be risky and catastrophic. Furthermore, financial markets believe in accumulation. When you're ready to retire, there is a common withdrawal plan based on the Trinity study—a 1998 paper written by three financial professors at Trinity University.

According to the paper, a person has sufficient savings when 4 percent of their assets can cover a year's expenses.[11] The financial markets don't focus on cash flow; rather, the goal is to get the biggest pile you can and then dig into the principal at retirement. In addition to investing in a risky endeavor, financial markets maintain a goal of accumulation followed by a lifetime of minimal depletions. This is not the formula for living a full, free life; it is based on scarcity and a zero-sum game.

Capital assets have many more benefits over paper (financial or

---

11   Philip L. Cooley, Carl M. Hubbard, and Daniel T. Walz, "Retirement Savings: Choosing a Withdrawal Rate That Is Sustainable," *AAII Journal* 10, no. 3 (1998): 16–21.

Wall Street) investments. Financial advisers don't offer alternative investments because they can't make a living selling them. Their livelihood is selling Wall Street products. It doesn't matter that those products only benefit Wall Street and the financial advisers and do very little for the client who believes that there are no other options.

I'm here to tell you, that whether you are young or old, green or experienced, there is an alternative way to look at life using capital assets that focuses on sustainable cash flow and growth, not depletion. The goal is that, no matter what amount a person starts with, that capital base will grow along with sustainable income. It's a totally different approach to retirement planning.

> I'm here to tell you, that whether you are young or old, green or experienced, there is an alternative way to look at life using capital assets that focuses on sustainable cash flow and growth, not depletion.

In my own experience, and in the experience of my clients, true freedom is derived from the predictability and sustainability of the cash flow rather than just relying on the acquisition and accumulation of a large capital base, which is what the financial markets do.

That's essentially what separates Wall Street investing from Main Street investing; those who like Wall Street like it because it takes no real work or expertise. It's an efficient market.

In an efficient market, like the stock market, everyone has the same information. In an efficient market, you buy at whatever the market price is. You can buy individual stocks or put your money in stock or bond funds, or you hand it over to a money manager and keep your fingers crossed. There is no legal way to buy stocks or bonds at a below-market price.

On the other hand, the real estate market is a perfect example of an inefficient market. Price setting is what the seller and buyer agree upon. It has little to do with the market at large. There is no efficient exchange (like NYSE) for real estate transactions.

It is much more advantageous to invest in an inefficient market because you have the capacity to have more information that the seller doesn't have that can make your investment worth a whole lot more than what the seller thinks it is worth. This is why there are no smoking bargains to be found on the Dow Jones but plenty down the street. However, this takes effort. It takes study and collaboration with others.

Capital assets offer more control, which does require responsibility. In this way, capital assets have a barrier to entry. Capital assets take work. There are a lot of moving parts. Real estate, specifically, is about insider information (no worries—this is completely legal), speed, and due diligence. Financial information is difficult to consume and further understand, and you have few eyes monitoring any one transaction. Not everyone has access to the same information, and even if they did, they don't know how to digest it.

With capital assets, you do not abdicate to a financial adviser and hope for the best. You do have to learn how capital assets work. You need to find knowledgeable people who can direct you to the right capital assets, because it's an inherently inefficient market.

There are two types of capital assets I discuss with clients—a real business (as discussed in chapter 4) and real estate. It doesn't matter if you invest in a house, a rental house, an apartment complex, or a self-storage facility, because they all have cash flow production behind them. As I mentioned, cash flow is the first thing I look at when I work with clients.

Real estate assets also provide certain tax preferences with depreciation offsets and lower long-term capital gains tax rate. You have the ability to exchange gains in capital assets to other investment assets (1031 exchange) and defer paying the current tax when you sell. You also maintain the ability to acquire multiple assets with less of your own money through financial leverage and other people's money.

Like anything, capital investing starts by informing yourself. This is achieved using the Freedom Assets we've already discussed—investing in yourself and your network. Through books, lectures, online resources, and people in your network, begin to educate yourself on business ownership and real estate. Rely on thought leaders around you to fill in any gaps you might have in your own knowledge. If you don't have time to invest in educating yourself, it is imperative that you build, maintain, and rely on a sound network.

Next, you need to be searching for access points—good opportunities in capital asset investments. These access points can be found through a network of specific people, masterminds, or brokers. This is why the key to capital assets is building your network.

Being in a community where other people are bringing information and resources can save you a lot of time. For this reason, invest in better, more productive relationships. If you can find a community like Freedom Founders, then you are on a fast track through these stages because we offer a community that has education, information, and knowledge.

You might be able to find local resources through real estate exchange meetings and similar groups that could provide you with further resources. These networks become your informal board of directors and can provide collaboration and future investment opportunities.

Investment plans are structured, customized plans based on your desired timeline for freedom. You need to consider current assets, debt, and available investment capital. Based on these conditions, you then need to balance risk with potential reward.

You must also consider income and growth. Some people need more income up front, while others prefer more growth. For people who desire to go faster, you might seek investments with higher potential for growth, still mitigating downside risk. Determine your income growth ratio and then find a suitable investment with the proper risk-adjusted returns to fit your profile.

Also be certain to assess your risk tolerance. For example, you may have a lower risk tolerance because you're not educated enough yet. You might start with low risk to gain experience before moving to higher growth or higher income potential. All of these customizations are what make alternative investments accessible to all people.

There's a wide variety of opportunity in capital investing, but you have to put yourself in the environment. You have to decide and then commit to investing in yourself, putting yourself in the environment, and identifying those access points to achieve freedom.

Alternative investments aren't passive. If you want to be passive, then hire a broker and put your money on Wall Street. Though the goal of capital investments is passive income, that is a misnomer because there's nothing inactive about it.

There are not many things that are made better by being passive. Consider your health or your relationships—would they be better if you were passive or active? Proactive or reactive? Your investments are the same way. You worked hard to earn your money, so why would you stop working to compound your money?

Because passive income is a myth, I prefer to use the term annuity income. Annuity is sustainable, regular, and predictable. That's what we want. Create or acquire the capital asset one time, and the *annuity income* continues in perpetuity.

Capital investing does take active involvement to acquire it and then invest it wisely. Just like investing in each of the Freedom Assets, you want to continue to stay involved with your investments. It does require more of you, but the benefit of getting to your Freedom Number sooner with a higher level of control is certainly worth it.

CASH FLOW INVESTMENTS KEYS TO SUCCESS:

1. Know your monthly burn rate (lifestyle overhead).

2. Know your Freedom Number (how much monthly income you need to equal or surpass your monthly lifestyle burn rate).

3. Have capital investments designed to create regular cash flow (versus accumulation).

4. Ensure that your investments are protected from sudden market disruption (downside risk adjustment).

5. Find access through your network to curated and vetted real estate investment opportunities that are of higher value than consumer-grade investments that are available to the masses.

6. Take control of your wealth and investments; make sure they're not tied up in 401(k)s or other restrictive investment vehicles.

If capital investment was easy, everybody would do it. You can't do what everybody else does and expect different outcomes. If you do what the majority does, you're going to have a mediocre life. You can't earn your way to freedom using the traditional work model. You must remember that if you want to *have* a different life, then you must *live* a different life.

For more information on how real estate investing can change your life, see my book *From High Income to High Net Worth for Dentists: The Ultimate Guide to Gain Freedom in Your Life with More Time Off, Less Stress, Security & Peace of Mind.*

HOW I'VE INVESTED IN MY CAPITAL

As I prepared for my first year of dental school in Dallas, I approached my father with a proposal: rather than pay rent for four years, what if he bought a rental property (because as a young student, I had little money) and I would manage it? My father didn't have much experience in real estate investing, but he recognized I had researched the market and had a sound plan.

After several lengthy discussions, he agreed. He traveled from Colorado to Dallas, and after visiting many potential listings, we purchased a house in 1980—we called it the Vanderbilt House because of its street name. He provided the financing, and I managed it.

I consider this my first joint venture with outside capital. Though I didn't have the money to invest, my part of that joint venture—my capital—was the time, the management. Though I wasn't receiving any money up front (cash flow), I knew I could expect back end growth, meaning I had potential to receive a chunk of money at some point when we harvested the equity by selling the property. After my graduation four years later, we sold the property and split a $50,000 capital gain profit.

During school, my active income was made by waiting tables on nights and weekends. After selling our property, I went back and calculated the number of hours I worked at restaurants over four years with the total dollars that I received. I then compared this dollar-per-hour earning with the capital gain growth in my real estate asset.

The real estate asset ended up being ten times more valuable per hour than waiting tables. Ten times! This was a huge moment for me. I realized that capital assets could outperform my best days trading my time for dollars. I knew I was on to something and had to keep going.

Since I had $25,000 in capital from the sale of the Vanderbilt House my dad and I shared, I immediately sought out ways to apply all I had learned about investing. I soon found a fourplex for sale and, with a combination of a down payment and seller financing, I was able to purchase the property without involving the bank. Within a few months, using the leverage of the fourplex, I bought a duplex. Not long after, I sought a single-family ranch-style house. Using that initial $25,000 profit, I now owned three properties.

Over the next fifteen years, using considerable leverage like taking over the seller's debt obligations and/or using seller financing, I parlayed the $25,000 profit from that first joint venture in real estate investment into another thirty-five rental properties. At that time, those properties created over $15,000 per month in annuity net income.

A NOTE ON PASSIVE INCOME:

Yes, *passive income* is widely overused. I prefer *annuity income*. Acquiring thirty-five rental properties required a good bit of my time. It was like running a part-time business. Since I did everything myself back then, I probably spent an average of three to four hours per week managing those investment assets and another thousand hours learning how to do it. For this reason, your time must be factored into your total returns.

However, this time is an investment that has lifetime benefits that are transferable to many other business and investment opportunities. With time and commitment, you can be your best investment adviser!

As I learned early in my investing career, capital assets allow for the use of financial leverage. The asset has a market value, and in capital assets, you can negotiate with motivated sellers to get lower acquisition prices. Leverage means you can put a smaller percentage of money down relative to the value of the sale price of the asset and use other people's money to finance the rest.

If you'd like to replace your active practice income with passive investment income within two to three years, and you have at least $1 million in available capital (can include residential / practice equity or practice sale), then go the following link to schedule a quick call with my team. If it looks like there is a mutual fit, you'll have the opportunity to schedule a call with me directly: FreedomFounders.com/Schedule.

Most of the time people think about other people's money as the bank. That's traditional, and it does work; however, I didn't go to the bank. I negotiated and got the sellers to finance a lot of their equity to me, and/or I took over their existing loans they already had in the property. I used some of my money to give them some down payment and then some of the money for property updates. This is a key advantage to capital investments: you can acquire more with less of your own money.

The average price of the thirty-five houses I owned was $75,000. If I had waited and saved up the money to buy houses, I would have maybe been able to buy two. But instead, as long as the cash flowed, I could keep pyramiding. Businesses are the same way. You can buy businesses with financing, and you build the business, add to the cash flow, and leverage it further. Creating cash flow is the key.

Even though I was leveraging buying properties, I had to make sure that the combination of the debt leveraging financing plus normal operating costs and management expenses were less than my gross rents. In other words, I had to have net cash flow because that's the whole purpose here. It's those few hundred dollars of net cash flow over and above the debt and expenses that make a capital asset work so well.

Once I had the cash flow, I took any extra money I had left over from my practice needs, family lifestyle needs, and taxes, and—instead of giving it to Wall Street or a 401(k) like most people do, I took the extra money and either bought more property or snow-balled the loans—meaning I was paying more than I was required to pay on the monthly principal and interest.

By snowballing, I could pay down a ten- or twenty-year amortized mortgage. I was knocking these down in five to seven years instead of ten to twenty years. This allowed me to attain free and clear capital assets—meaning no debt owed on them—within a relatively short period of time.

Within fifteen years, most of my thirty-five properties were free and clear. The reason this is important is because now the properties are producing a lot more cash flow than when I had to service the debt or was paying down more debt. That's what created my annuity cash flow so that I could hit my Freedom Number.

■ ■ ■

When I was sitting in the hospital with my child, I knew she was the answer to *why* I wanted freedom. Without time to analyze my finances, annuity cash flow, and Freedom Number, I might never have formulated my *how*. The *why* and the *how* are the keys to building a Freedom Lifestyle.

My *why* was Jenna, and my *how* were the capital investments that produced sustainable annuity income, giving me the stability that I needed to be able to sell my dental practice. Had I been investing in the traditional financial model of accumulation, I would not have had that confidence and could not have sold the practice to be able to spend time with Jenna. The key is not to try to maintain a high just-in-case Freedom Number; it's to specifically know *why* that's your number and *how* you're going to get there.

Understanding how to create wealth through capital assets is the path to financial freedom. If I built in that extra margin like traditional financial planners do, then it would have been a barrier to me getting to a Freedom Lifestyle sooner. It would have prolonged it. For me, I needed freedom right then and there, and I had devised a way to achieve it.

> **Understanding how to create wealth through capital assets is the path to financial freedom.**

Had I not taken the time to consider my *why* and *how*, I would have kept working hard with no end in sight, building, building, working, working, stacking up more assets. I finally asked myself the most important question of all: *When is enough, enough?*

Thanks to my daughter, I had a reason to ask myself that question, and its answer changed everything. This is why your Freedom Number is so important. It has the potential to change your life.

The traditional financial models tell you you're a long way away, so just keep on working, working, working. With the Freedom Number clearly defined, if you're not quite there yet, you know how close you are. Trust me—you're closer than you think.

Orchestrating your financial future does require discipline and education. However, if you desire true freedom sooner—not later—then the effort is a cause worth pursuing. It's a choice. You have to decide.

TAKEAWAYS:

- Freedom is about having choices and options. Restricted choices lead to restricted lives.

- You need "think time" to analyze your monthly spending and determine your Freedom Number—the monthly passive income amount required to replace your lifestyle burn rate.

- If we fail to invest at all, or if we fail to invest wisely, then we limit our future choices. For this reason, you need to put money toward capital investments.

- By educating yourself and building a network, you can position yourself to identify access points in an inefficient market—opportunities for capital asset investments.

- Capital investing does take active involvement to acquire it and then invest it wisely. Just like investing in each of the Freedom Assets, you want to continue to stay involved with your investments.

- Capital asset acquisition allows for financial leverage—the ability to acquire more assets using other people's money. This is a key wealth builder.

CHAPTER 7

Invest in Your Legacy

The purpose of life is not to be happy. It is to be useful, to be honorable, to be compassionate, to have it make some difference that you have lived and lived well.

—Ralph Waldo Emerson

■ ■ ■

The majority of our Freedom Founders members who have gone through the Freedom Blueprint process shift their focus from a scarcity mindset—focusing on making enough to pay the bills—to one of legacy building. Most people think of legacy as planning estates, transferring assets, and drafting wills and trusts. This is certainly a part of investing in your legacy, but there are bigger pieces.

Legacy is of greater value than tangible assets. It's more about who you are, how you show up, and what wisdom you're transmitting to the next generation—starting with your family.

One of our Freedom Founders couples is in their early sixties with two adult children. As a part of their legacy, they have started encouraging their children to take additional steps now—like creating outside sources of income—so that they can achieve freedom sooner. They want their children to have the time and peace of mind to spend more relational time with their own young families.

Though both adult children are on traditional career paths, the parents hope to offer them an alternate path by sharing their own wisdom, experiences, and resources. The couple is now transferring some of what they have learned about the Freedom Blueprint process to their children—this is legacy.

As this couple learned, when you reach your Freedom Number and have replaced the active income your family requires, it doesn't mean you quit; rather, you advance to another level and a more purpose-driven life. As we learned in chapter 2 through Maslow's hierarchy of needs, you cannot free up the time and mental space to think about your legacy until you transition from a deficiency mindset to an abundance mindset.

A Freedom Lifestyle means you shift focus from fulfilling the basic, fundamental necessities of life to cultivating a life of significance and meaning that you can pass forward. Not only does this shift have a positive effect on future generations; it brings profound purpose to your life.

Hitting your Freedom Number means you have the opportunity to think about some of the broader questions in life: Who am I? What am I really about? What do I want to teach other people? What am I doing right now that's significant and will carry on past my time? The answers to those questions are your legacy.

For this couple, their legacy included introducing their adult children to the counterculture of Freedom Founders. Since then, the children have attended several meetings and understand there are alternate pathways to career and wealth building.

Though they are already on their career paths, they don't want stagnancy and are therefore open to taking some risks. Too many people, especially those in midlife, get stuck in a fear-based mindset. Work becomes about making money; life becomes about spending money, and a cycle begins that keeps them trapped in the traditional work model for decades.

What these adult children are receiving as part of their legacy is the permission to explore alternate models. What a gift this is! As I've learned in my own life, it's okay to try something different. It's okay to be a renegade.

Typically we measure success by a person's career path, finances, and lifestyle. This is why when I talk about a Freedom Lifestyle, many people think only of financial freedom. It's the safety net, the certainty that one can retire. This is the traditional mindset I aspire to change.

Of course financial freedom is important, but it is not the end goal. It's not just about building bigger businesses or making millions of dollars. It's about having purpose.

We all want to be successful; we want to provide for our families and measure our achievements by dollars. That's human. But at the end of the day—at the end of your life—whose life have you made better? Why do you do what you do? What impact are you having in your family, your community? What kind of generational legacy are you leaving?

You have to be purposeful and intentional about your legacy. People often think legacy is what you *leave*, but legacy is actually what you *live*. Every day, either by design or default, you are living out your legacy.

You have to keep legacy in mind daily so that it dictates your actions, choices, and behaviors. When you are not intentional about your legacy, then by default you're leaving a void to be filled in by society at large—including the traditional model of work and wealth. If you're not doing it intentionally, then you're abdicating your responsibility and your purpose.

People usually don't start to think about aspects of legacy until they are faced with their mortality. But why wait until death?

Like the Freedom Founders couple realized, you have the most influence today. This couple demonstrated how investing doesn't end when you are financially free. In fact, in some ways that is when the most valuable investing begins.

Don't wait until later to invest in your legacy. Start doing it now so you can have the greatest influence on your family, your community, and your world.

WHAT'S MY RESPONSIBILITY?

Too often we think of legacy as the amount of money left behind, but investing in your legacy is not limited to the money you offer others. Sure, being able to write a check to an organization doing good work is beneficial and can certainly be part of your legacy. However, I want you to start thinking of the other resources you might also be able to offer.

Legacy is not only what you have left behind for your family; it's also about the sustainable programs and opportunities you created to better the community around you. It's about the insights you impart to future generations that offer them alternative pathways to living.

If there is a group or organization in line with your values, for example, get involved on a ground level. You can give money and/ or be part of their work mission. You can mentor others who are searching for the guidance of experienced individuals. Oftentimes it's your time and expertise that can be most helpful to others, so get in the mix.

Anybody who has lived a good life has the responsibility to give back their time, money, knowledge, or experience. There are endless ways to serve others. Sure, you can travel to other countries and volunteer at orphanages or build wells, but if you have children, your legacy should start at home. Taking small intentional moments to connect with your children teaches them about their own value and worth. It also creates a model for how they treat others and the kinds of connections they will seek out.

From there, you can cast a wider net and consider what you can do for your communities—at work, where you live, and in the world at large. You can volunteer at libraries or schools. You can find a national organization in your area and write a check or offer you time. There are so many ways you can get involved and be a part of something bigger than yourself.

Too often we don't invest time and effort into our legacies because we are too busy. Maybe you can't attend mission trips or spend a week digging irrigation trenches or build houses for your neighbors, but you can *intentionally* grab hold of small moments and make them significant.

Also remember that you don't have to hit your Freedom Number to invest in your legacy. There are small things you can start doing today to create the habit of a purposeful life.

At Freedom Founders, we encourage all members to maintain an attitude of service. Whether you have ten dollars or ten million dollars, you can start to ask yourself each day who you can serve that day. This shift in mindset has profound effects on the individuals and teams you interact with. These small acts of service start to build your legacy and make the world better.

When people within our group do hit their Freedom Number, they become Free for Life. At that point, part of their opportunity and responsibility is to provide service hours to their own community and to the Freedom Founders community. Because the people have garnered experiences and wisdom that could benefit others and build lasting legacies, our Free for Life members are often the leaders of our groups.

In this way, Freedom Founders is a microcosm of peer mentoring. It is our hope that in the same way members use their experience and expertise to help other members, so too will they mentor and lead their families and communities.

Understanding who you are on a deeper level than what you do allows you to separate yourself from your own ego. If you have never explored your purpose, significance, and meaning, it can be a barrier to deciding your next.

A great way to explore these deeper personal elements is to give back to those around you. This small change can make a big difference in how you transition from an active career to one that allows more time, freedom, and purpose.

Oftentimes, when people leave their careers and are no longer doing the thing, they feel insignificant in society. That doesn't need to be true. In fact, it's at this point in your life when you have the *most* to offer.

Our culture is youth based, and much of our motivation stems from what we can tangibly produce. As soon as that's over, society says, "You're done." When you are involved in serving others, however, you realize there is so much value in experience and in being able to give back. If legacy and meaning are left unexplored, it's a missed opportunity to find the value in all you've learned and lived.

FROM THE HEART

Investing in legacy doesn't always come easy. Oftentimes, the most challenging aspect is identifying in what unique ways you can contribute to others. As I was working on this chapter, Kandace and I hosted a couple in our home for their Freedom Blueprint Day. Both spouses were dentists in a unique concierge-type practice they built.

When I asked the husband about the aspects of his work he liked best, he said it was mentoring associate doctors. As we were discussing alternative ways to produce income, I pointed out that they had built a truly inventive practice. Rather than be managed by insurance codes and reimbursements, they had created a business where the exchange of value was revered. I encouraged them to explore this further by creating a small "over the shoulders" program to teach other practitioners how to replicate this model.

They responded like many people do when thinking about legacy: "But we don't have the credentials to do that." I laughed. "Your experiences *are* your credentials." You don't need more degrees or certificates on the wall to share something of value with others. If you've *done* something, then you can transfer your wisdom and teach it to others.

When I was contemplating my own exit from my dental practice, I too had trouble understanding what I could offer outside of dentistry. What was my next? For some time, I didn't know because

I couldn't see what I could offer of value. I knew dentistry and I had developed a propensity for real estate investing, but I didn't see the relevance or the connection. We all have blind spots to our own valuable attributes. Luckily, I had people around me who helped me put the pieces together.

I admit that for too long I was chasing wealth. I didn't have time to think about my next or my legacy. Once I got to that place where I felt more secure and grounded, my attitude and perspective changed. I started to think more about what I could leave that would have a lasting effect.

Once I sold my practice, I had the time and freedom to attend various conferences. I liked going to marketing conferences and real estate conferences, and one day I learned of an upcoming public speaking conference.

As I mentioned, I had never done public speaking because I never wanted to. I had never talked to any groups. I did revere, however, the power of communication and thought it couldn't hurt to learn more about those skills. I said to my wife, "Why don't we go do this?" She agreed, and we went to our first public speaking conference.

As you can imagine, the facilitator was quite charismatic. He talked about the trade of communication, or speaking for a living, which I had never considered. Outside the conference, he led a coaching program that helped attendees construct businesses around speaking skills. Out of curiosity and an interest in the power of storytelling, I signed up.

In working with him, he mentioned that I had a unique combination of skills in dentistry and real estate. I didn't see that at all. They seemed like disparate interests that had nothing to do with the other. Though it would take some time for me to see what that coach saw, I understood his outside perspective gave me clarity. There are some things in life you cannot do alone, and finding your next can be one of those areas.

I also learned during that conference what I feared to be true: I was a terrible speaker. I remember the facilitator constantly reminding me, "You've got to start speaking from the heart. Speak from the heart!" The heart? No way. I lived in my head. I was always analyzing, observing.

With time, practice, and more reminders to speak from my heart, I learned to be more comfortable in my communication. Soon I realized that I did have a story, and perhaps, like most stories, it was worth sharing. Better yet, when I was authentic and present in my communication, I spoke from the heart.

The more I shared, the more confident I became that communication was part of my legacy. No one was more shocked about this than I was. In 2010, I hosted a small group of dentists at my home to share how I had used real estate investments to attain my goals. With the unique skills and experience I had acquired, I led my colleagues toward something they were all chasing—freedom.

Like them, I had found that trading time for dollars wasn't getting me closer to freedom. On purpose—but without a clear design—I had figured out a plan B through real estate that allowed me to build more wealth and eventual cash flow than all the years working in my dental practice.

This initial event led to a lot of trial and error. But at least I started someplace. First I rented out small hotel rooms for groups of twenty people, to present on real estate. Then I decided I would try to do some larger, multispeaker events. Every event was not a home run, though I was putting a fair amount of time and investment into it. There wasn't much return other than the personal satisfaction of helping people. I hadn't yet figured out the model, but I persevered, buoyed by the feeling that I was aligning myself with my greater purpose and legacy.

When several of the Freedom Founders couples became Free for Life using my method, that's when the idea really cemented that I could leave a legacy for other families. Each time I worked with a new couple or gave a new talk, I continued to adapt and evolve. Eventually, I felt like a competent speaker, teacher, and coach with a story to share (from the heart, of course), so I started writing books.

I'm now fulfilling my purpose and working on my legacy, which is a great feeling. Every day I wake up inspired because I look at my schedule, and I like what I see. It's my choice. I am spending time with people I enjoy, discussing topics I love.

When I was a dentist, I enjoyed the 20 percent of my schedule that allowed me to interact with patients. The other 80 percent was "had to" time doing the things I "had to" do. It wasn't fun, but I was locked into the traditional model that precluded any other options.

Today, it's 100 percent fun. That's freedom—doing what you want to do, when you want to do it, with whom you want to do it, where you want to do it.

Today, Freedom Founders boasts over 70 current members with more than 150 people having participated in some aspect of our program. My own next included becoming a speaker, coach, author, and (self-proclaimed) contrarian thought leader. The goal was never to create Freedom Founders as an extension of myself; rather, I want to share proven strategies with others so they, too, can enjoy full freedom.

WHAT REMAINS

It's no surprise that the older we get, the more we think about legacy and purpose. I know the impetus for my own path began when my daughter was fighting for her life in the hospital. I thought of it again after my mother passed unexpectedly in 2001. When my father was diagnosed with esophageal cancer in 2017, I had the opportunity to talk with him about the impermanence of life and what remains after we're gone.

In fact, not long after his diagnosis, my father came to a Freedom Founders event and agreed to join me on stage for a recorded conversation about what he'd learned in his life:

> David Phelps (DP): "Having lived a long, full life, what is one of the most important lessons you've learned?"

> Herschel Phelps (HP): "I think one of the really important lessons in life is being true to yourself. I think so many people act according to what people expect of you, or want of you, and it's a big mistake to let other people control your life in that way."

> DP: "Fourteen years ago, you had to make a transition that most people fear, when Mom passed away unexpectedly. She was in the prime of her life; you were in the prime of your life. In Freedom Founders, we talk a lot about not waiting for *someday* to enjoy life. Can you talk a little bit about that transition? Because we all may face that at some point."

> HP: "It was difficult for me to adjust. I realized soon after my wife died that the person I was died with her. I had to figure out, *Who am I without my partner of forty-eight*

years? When you've been together that long, you really become part of each other. The person I had been was gone. I had to figure out who I was without her and what my purpose was."

DP: "What advice would you give for dealing with things like this that are outside of one's control?"

HP: "That's a difficult one. All you can do is make your choices and decisions with the best information you have available. You can't beat yourself up for something that, in retrospect, didn't turn out as well as it might have."

DP: "How do you want to be remembered?"

HP: "I want to be remembered as a kind person, a thoughtful person—someone who left the world better than it would've been without my input."

My father seemed to inherently understand from a young age that legacy is built daily. Every interaction he had with me, or in my presence, informed the kind of legacy he left for me.

My father was an eye surgeon, so I oftentimes accompanied him on his weekend rounds at the hospital. Even in his routine work environment, I remember seeing how my father acknowledged each person he saw at the hospital. Whether he saw custodians, doctors, nurses, or cafeteria staff, he acknowledged them and gave them his full attention.

He didn't just build a legacy in his work environment; whether he was paying for gas or ordering food, he took time to authentically connect with the person before him. Sometimes that might just be a short, simple conversation, but it made an impression on others—

especially me—and contributed to his legacy and my own.

With each interaction, my father made someone else's life better—if only for a moment—because he made them feel seen, heard, and valued. This was his purpose, and he did, in fact, leave the world a better place, just as he hoped.

It's not common for young people to think critically about their legacy. At a young age, most of us are following the traditional path of accumulation—accumulating education, training, debt, salaries, homes, cars. There are a million things we are right in the middle of.

This mentality of rushing from one responsibility to another does a disservice to ourselves, our families, our communities, and our legacies. As my father taught me, it's the small moments that hold the greatest potential for connection.

What impedes legacy building? Concerning yourself with what others will think of you. Legacy is not about what we leave for people but what we leave *in* them. If you don't pass on your life experience by leaving a legacy, the wisdom you've gained through decades of difficult learning will disappear as your physical body wears out.

> Legacy is not about what we leave for people but what we leave *in* them.

Your legacy is not something you put on a tombstone—it's what you're doing today, how you're serving, how you're communicating with other people in your relationships. You're building that legacy right now.

If you wait to think about your legacy until you reach the end, you've waited too long. I understand the fear of death. Spoiler alert: it's real. It's actually out there. We can't stop it, but we can talk about it, understand it, prepare for it.

Legacy is about life, not death. Legacy isn't tomorrow. Legacy is now, today. How people think of you *now* is how people will think of you *then*. Legacy goes far beyond society's definition of "success," which is all about "me" and says nothing about how we serve others.

The things we do for ourselves are gone when we are gone, but the things we do for others remain as our legacy. You won't be remembered for the work that you do unless that work changed the lives of others.

Everyone leaves a legacy, either by intention or default. With blessings come great responsibilities. Building a legacy is arguably the most powerful thing you can do in your life because it enables you to have influence well into the future.

TAKEAWAYS:

- Take the time to explore who you are and what your strengths and unique abilities are.
- Don't follow the path of the majority. Be true to yourself.
- You can't live life as a soloist. You need trusted people to help guide you toward the life and legacy you hope to build.
- Maintain an attitude of service.
- Concerning yourself with what others will think of you blocks legacy building.

CHAPTER 8

Free for Life

After years of tirelessly working hard in my small dental practice, I was in a dark place. I wasn't happy doing what I was doing, and I was looking for something different.

I always heard colleagues say they would sell their practice one day and live off the earnings. That was never a potential reality for me. I was ready to get out now, not one day.

Then I found Freedom Founders. After our first workshop, it was obvious that it was the right path for my wife and me. Since we joined, my perspective on investing and finances is different. I feel blessed to have this group. It's a powerful thing to have smart people—who I know and trust—weighing in on my investments and my strategies.

Our Freedom Blueprint Day with David and Kandace was incredibly valuable. The next week, I started taking an extra day off a week. In the last couple months, we've had two of the most productive days we've had in the whole time that I've been practicing.

I'm excited to go into work now. I'm excited to see my staff. We give high fives in my office, and we continue to have record months.

To be financially free is a great thing, especially at this point in my children's lives. They're the most important things to us. Freedom of time is going to do so much for our family. These are precious times I won't ever get back, so I don't want to miss anything.

—Dr. Ben Jensen

■ ■ ■

Let's get real: the traditional wealth-building model is failing. Professional practitioners like Dr. Jensen are diligently working only to discover that the dream has failed them, and the retirement they were promised is still beyond reach. Everyone shares the same goal of complete freedom, but not everyone knows how to get there.

The goal of the Freedom Founders Blueprint program is to help members become Free for Life—an honor that signifies that the member has reached full freedom and can live with all options available to them to determine what's next.

We have helped nine members reach this milestone, with almost that same number prepared to achieve it within the next year. Though the Freedom Founders network has been available to support these members through the process, there are two common barriers that block many people from achieving their own freedom.

1. WHAT'S MY NUMBER?

The first hindrance to freedom is financial. The question that everybody asks, whether they're a Freedom Founders member or not, is "Do I have enough money to leave my job, and will it sustain me for the remainder of my life?" To overcome the financial obstacle on your path to freedom, you have to understand the difference between the traditional model and the Freedom Founders model.

The traditional model fails greatly because it's based on accumulation. Having enough or not having enough is an arbitrary approximation based on accumulation: How much capital investment can you stack up?

Using the traditional model, a financial planner would quote a professional practice owner used to living on a significant six-figure income to save $6, $8, or $10 million dollars. You read that right—*$6 to $10 million dollars!* How does the math work? At a 3 percent withdrawal or depletion rate, $6 million allows for $180,000 per year before tax; $10 million allows for $300,000 of lifestyle income before tax. That sounds like a pretty solid retirement lifestyle.

There's just one problem: how many hardworking professionals do you believe can aggregate $6 to $10 million in savings through traditional 401(k) retirement accounts, whole life insurance policies, or index funds by the age of sixty-five? Very few. It's a rare feat for highly compensated technicians to save this much, so the average worker barely has a chance to achieve freedom.

What if you could have financial freedom with far less accumulated savings? It's possible, but it requires a different model than most have learned. Are you contrarian, or do you follow the majority?

The Freedom Founders Blueprint model is based on a Freedom Number—the monthly *cash flow* number you need to live on. The

Freedom Number is not millions of dollars; it's however much you need monthly (grossed up for taxes). Our focus in on the capital asset value you need to produce a certain amount of recurring dollars per month.

It's like having a golden goose, and rather than eating the golden goose—which does you no good—you invest in its care so that it produces continuous rewards. The Freedom Founders method is based on sustainable, predictable cash flow, and this is what's missing from traditional financial planning. It's the uncertainty of not knowing—not having a viable number—that keeps many professionals fearful of going Free for Life.

2. WHAT'S MY NEXT?

For many people, once they know their Freedom Number and they see a pathway to get there by acquiring enough (or investing in enough) capital assets, the next obstacle they face is an existential one: they must figure out who they are outside of labels like "dentist" or "doctor." Oftentimes, not having an office to go to, a staff to manage, or patients to see makes technicians lose their identity and grapple with some larger questions: *What am I going to do now? What's my next?*

It's quite common for a person to self-sabotage at this point in the process. If I offer them next steps to find a buyer for their practice, for example, they might subconsciously delay the steps or procrastinate in taking them. This is often because of fear. People don't know what life looks like when they aren't doing the thing they were trained to do. It feels like a void, and golf can only fill up so much of a person's time!

The best way to fill the space is through community. This is why

I formed Freedom Founders—to offer a collaborative community for networking, advice, and support. What we help people do is to focus on the top level of the Five Freedoms—significance, meaning, and purpose.

When you live a life focused on these higher elements, then you have a new perspective. You're no longer expending so much time, effort, and energy financially caring for yourself and your family. Now those resources can be diverted to building your legacy and answering "What's my next?"

It's important to remember that with the right coaching and support, you can overcome these two common obstacles and become Free for Life. For most people who are in the later stages of their careers, they are within three to five years of being financially capable of exiting or transitioning out of their careers. That's right: three to five years. Let that sink in. Believe me, you're closer than you think.

3. HOW DO I BECOME FREE FOR LIFE?

The Freedom Founders Blueprint model is unique—there's nothing like it anywhere. It's based on integrity and organic relationships, speed and implementation. It's for those who are willing to buck the traditional accumulation model and take ownership of their futures. Let's take a closer look at the process that Freedom Founders members work through to become Free for Life.

STEPS TO BECOMING FREE FOR LIFE:

1. Personal key assessment
2. Assess liabilities and debt
3. Determine available capital to invest

4. Assess nonnegotiables

5. Define freedom

6. Determine Freedom Number

7. Practice and investments assessments

8. Create Freedom Blueprint

9. Free for Life application

Personal Key Assessment

As part of the initial assessment for Freedom Founders members, we measure them in financial and nonfinancial areas. The purpose of these assessments is to help me future pace them. Even though they haven't achieved freedom yet, I want them to start thinking about it. I want them to visualize what it will look like for them. The goal is to create transparency from the beginning so we can build them a Freedom Blueprint.

1. How much longer I *want* to practice: I would say _____ years.

2. How much longer I will likely *have* to practice: I would say _____ years.

3. What am I willing to do to change? Am I willing to possibly sacrifice in the short term for long-term freedom? Are my family and spouse on board?

4. My financial and real estate acumen: How comfortable do I feel about investments in general and/or real estate investment?

5.   Risk tolerance: Using leverage (debt) versus con-
     servative low or no debt (accumulation theory), do
     I have low risk tolerance or high risk tolerance? Or
     somewhere in between?

Assess Liabilities and Debt

Next, I ask members to perform an assessment of current debt liabilities and delineate which debts should be prioritized to be paid down (or off) first. I know this a hard moment for some people, but you can't create a Freedom Blueprint until you are honest with yourself about where you currently are.

CURRENT DEBT LIABILITIES		
A. Short term (credit cards, line of credit, car loan—anything five years or less)		
ACCOUNT OR TYPE OF DEBT	CURRENT BALANCE	MONTHLY PAYMENT
1.	$	$
2.	$	$
3.	$	$
4.	$	$

B. Long term (real estate mortgages, student loans—anything more than five years)		
ACCOUNT OR TYPE OF DEBT	**CURRENT BALANCE**	**MONTHLY PAYMENT**
1.	$	$
2.	$	$
3.	$	$
4.	$	$

Determine Available Capital to Invest

Next, I ask for a full inventory of your assets—whether you like them or not, whether they are good investments or not. It doesn't matter if you want to access them at all for alternative investments—that can be determined later.

Right now, you just need to inventory. The goal is to see what investments or equities are currently underinvested and could be redeployed into better investments. This also includes looking at the person's current retirement account assets, which we call "buckets" of money or investments.

There are three types of financial buckets. The first bucket of money holds common taxable financial accounts—stocks, bonds, mutual funds, and annuities. The second bucket of money holds the equity from real estate or businesses. The third bucket would be monies in retirement accounts.

THREE BUCKETS OF MONEY:

1. Taxable financial accounts (stocks, bonds, mutual funds, annuities)

2. Equity in real estate or businesses

3. Retirement accounts (includes cash value life insurance that is tax free to heirs)

Which of your buckets are full? And which ones are empty? People typically have taxable accounts or cash value in life insurance. Many times people also have some traditional retirement accounts or IRAs. Ideally, they also have equity in real estate and/or businesses— their home, office building, or practice.

Remember, your dollars should work as hard for you as you worked for them. We want them to work to their fullest potential.

Assess Nonnegotiables

What are your nonnegotiables? What will you absolutely not sacrifice on the path to freedom? Some Freedom Founders members, for example, have said they want to stay in their current home, their city, or their school district. Some have said they will not expend any more of their time. Some have an annual family vacation they will not cancel or a vacation home they want to keep.

It's nice to return to this list after we formulate their Freedom Blueprint and talk to them frankly about what they want. For example, they might want to be out of their active income in three years, and it's not looking feasible. Oftentimes, I can refer to this list and tell them that unless they are willing to negotiate, then their three-year timeline is unattainable. The entire process is about getting real with yourself.

When you have a definitive goal—a milepost—of three more years until freedom, for example, then it changes your perspective. If I can get them to visualize their freedom and fully understand how the Blueprint gets them there, then they're likely to make bigger decisions than they would if it was an intangible *one day*.

Financial advising doesn't have to be complicated. With the traditional model, it's all abstract. It seems so far away. You don't know what you're giving up, and you don't know what you're getting.

It's like playing *The Price is Right*, with all the prizes behind curtains. Bob Barker asks, "Would you give up what's behind curtain A to get what is behind curtain B?" How would you know? It's pure speculation.

What if he said, "Would you give up your blender to receive a car?" You *know* the answer to that one. So, sure, maybe you don't want to forgo your annual three-week vacation to Maui, but if you were told that by doing so, you could achieve financial freedom two years earlier, you might change your mind. "I'll take two years, Bob!"

Define Freedom

It's important that you start to visualize and explore what freedom looks like for you. I want you to do this for two reasons—to spare you an identity crisis and to give you motivation.

First, you need to look ahead and visualize a day much sooner than you were prepared for. You need to think about how you will spend your time and what will give you purpose. Too often when people achieve freedom, their ego is in crisis because they don't know who they are outside of their label.

Second, being able to picture your life, your time, and your family is a powerful motivator to get you to the finish line. For many people, they have never allowed themselves to think about their freedom because they thought it was unattainable. If it's not an option, it's too painful to even consider.

Now, it's an option. It's closer than you think. Take time to explore exactly what freedom means for you and your family.

YOUR DEFINITION OF FREEDOM:

- What do you do?
- How do you act?
- Do you do any active work? If so, what?
- Who do you spend time with?
- What are you passionate about—really passionate?
- What gives meaning in your life?
- What challenges you, if anything?

Assess Your Freedom Number

Now it's time to determine your Freedom Number based on your current monthly lifestyle "burn rate," or overhead. How much does it take to fund your family's lifestyle, including your current debt obligations or future obligations, such as children's education or other special needs considerations?

This is never considered to be a final or maximum number—this is the "get out of jail" number. The lower the Freedom Number, the easier and faster it is to be Free for Life (or pay off debt, prepare for special needs like college education, provide for elderly parents, etc.).

FREEDOM NUMBER:

What is your lifestyle overhead (burn rate)? What do you need in monthly cash flow before tax to maintain your desired or required lifestyle? (Multiply by 1.33 to gross up for taxes.)

Here's an example: the range of lifestyle burn rate in our Freedom Founders' group after tax is $16,000 to $22,000 per month. If we choose the median, $19,000 per month, and multiply by 1.33 to gross up for taxes, that equals $25,270 per month before tax.

Practice and Investments Assessments

By doing an assessment of both practice (current business) and current investments, you can identify your leverage possibilities—or inflection points.

We want to identify where your highest value leverage points are in these two categories. It's a place to start, and it helps you focus on which steps are highest priority to help you achieve freedom faster.

PRACTICE OPTIMIZATION ASSESSMENT:

Thinking about your current practice, rate each category on a scale of 1–10 (1 equals strongly disagree, and 10 equals strongly agree).

1. Too doctor dependent: Too dependent on dentist or owner—no culture, vision, leadership team

2. Sales and operations deficient: Inadequate sales training of staff and doctor, lack of incoming leads and conversion of treatment to current patients— phones and in person

3. Marketing deficient: No marketing strategy or continuity—website, landing pages, newsletter, social media, and so on. Lack of retention and reactivation process or regular touchpoint marketing. Lack of referral system.

4. Managed care insurance dependent: Reduced profit margins and increased overhead. Resorting to competing on price with volume.

5. Corporate clinic competition: Competition from Wall Street roll ups. Branding, marketing, and consumer hours. How do you compete?

6. Associates and partners potential: A developed plan B transition plan. When and how—creating an environment that competes with corporate for associates.

PASSIVE CASH FLOW WEALTH BUILDING: "HOW MUCH DO I NEED TO RETIRE?"

Thinking about your current cash flow and investments, rate each category on a scale of 1–10 (1 equals strongly disagree, and 10 equals strongly agree).

1. Excessive lifestyle overhead: Entitlement attitude? Keeping up with society or industry standards? At what cost? Cars, mansions, private school, college education.

2.   Insufficient net worth: Growth of asset base not on schedule for target freedom date

3.   Net worth growth inconsistent: No consistent increase in net worth year over year. Practice growth at plateau or decreasing value. Outside wealth building not on schedule.

4.   Investments not optimized: Net worth not optimized to produce maximum passive cash flow and/or hedge against future inflation—loss of dollar purchasing power in future years creates fear of being free.

5.   Practice at plateau: Little if any increase in value and/or cash flow profit from the practice.

6.   High taxation: No plan to mitigate for current and future higher confiscatory tax rates.

For a personalized Retirement Scorecard that measures your investing against industry benchmarks and offers personalized recommendations, go to FreedomFounders. com/Scorecard to take a three-minute assessment.

Create a Freedom Blueprint

The Freedom Blueprint is the bedrock of our process and serves as a road map on the path to freedom. It is created *with* clients in a one-day, one-on-one Freedom Blueprint consult with me and Kandace at our home. By the time people come for their consult, they have put all their think time in, they've assessed their situations, and they've started actively optimizing their practices.

When we consult with clients, we put three pieces of the process together—their personal component, practice assets, and capital assets. The personal side of their finances include their debt and their nonnegotiables. For most clients, their primary asset is their practice. This is where they earn their active income, and they're trying to optimize that. Outside the practice, we help them identify alternative investments in real estate that add to their capital assets.

There are two components to the capital investments: income and growth. Some investments are focused only on income, others are more focused on growth, and some are hybrid in that they provide income and growth. In developing a Freedom Blueprint for someone who wants to go Free for Life, the focus is on the income component, since that is what ultimately gains their freedom.

Free for Life Application

Freedom Founders members who have gone through the Freedom Blueprint process have made their investments, optimized their practices, and invested in the Five Freedoms—themselves, their business, their relationships, their capital, and their legacy.

Once they hit their Freedom Number, we offer them the opportunity to apply for Free for Life status. The process includes a comprehensive application along with a video submission that is reviewed by a team of financial leaders.

Part of what we are looking for is ensuring that the applicants are by our definition and their own Free for Life. We look for a 15 to 20 percent margin above their Freedom Number that is sustainable. Sometimes the team might need more information, so we ask for further documents or explanations. If we do not approve their status, we make a video explaining why and offer them one more chance in the future. Our clients report that this video is helpful for them to determine in what area they need to focus.

For people who are approved, the process gives them peace of mind that they are indeed ready for a Freedom Lifestyle. It's oftentimes a hard leap to make, so having a team of professionals objectively agree validates for members that they are ready to stop their active income.

SAMPLE FREE FOR LIFE APPLICATION QUESTIONS:

1. What is your definition of freedom?

2. Where are you on your path to Financial Freedom?

3. How comfortable are you with your current investment income?

4. What is your current annual lifestyle overhead (or burn rate)? Gross annual lifestyle overhead grossed up by 25 percent for taxes.

5. Do you have enough annual investment income to cover your lifestyle overhead?

6. Can you maintain (or increase) your investment cash flow without diminishing your principal long term?

7. Are you still generating active income (trading time for dollars)?

8. How much active income are you earning?

9. What concerns you most about your future?

10. What are your dreams and vision for the next five years? Ten years?

WHAT'S OUR NEXT?

No matter where you are today, you can take a step closer to your Freedom Lifestyle. I am fortunate to call author Dan Kennedy a mentor, and he continually inspires people to never let a dream die without extraordinary effort. In his autobiography, *My Unfinished Business*, he says, "I believe you are never too old, never too young, never too poor, never too anything to be required to give up on your dreams. Most people who make a lifelong practice of giving up on their dreams, ideas and opportunities wind up mastering only one skill: excuse-making, so they have a long, comforting list of reasons why they have not done more with life. I prefer achievement."[12]

Don't fall prey to giving up on your quest for freedom. No matter where you are today, remember you are closer to your Freedom Lifestyle than you think.

TAKEAWAYS:

- Have the certainty of a recurring cash flow Freedom Number instead of the traditional financial model that favors an accumulation number.

- Know the keys to your Freedom Blueprint: your nonnegotiables and lifestyle considerations, business assets, and capital assets.

- Being Free for Life doesn't stop when you reach your Freedom Number. It starts there but ends at the top of the Freedom Asset pyramid with the greatest rewards—peace of mind, security, meaning, and purpose.

---

12 Dan S. Kennedy, *My Unfinished Business* (Charleston: Advantage Media Group, 2009), 233.

What's Your Next?

One of my Freedom Founders members is a general practitioner of medicine in his early sixties. At his recent Blueprint Day with Kandace and me in our home, he brought along his wife and his twenty-two-year-old daughter, Laura. Laura recently obtained her undergraduate degree, and though she has enrolled in medical school, she opted to take a year off first.

When I asked Laura why she had taken a year off, she referenced her music experience and the travel opportunities it afforded her. She explained that she knew medicine would offer her a good foundation, much like it had her father, but she said, "I just wonder what else is out there." I gave Laura a copy of the book I'd written for young people called *The Apprentice Model* and told her that in it I encourage young people to take some time off before plunging into a career. I thought she was wise to take a year and consider the paths before her.

As we talked more, we brainstormed ways that she could use her music to make active income while she apprenticed with business leaders. We also arranged for her to attend our Freedom Blueprint Workshop as an intern to further cultivate her understanding of our freedom-based approach to wealth and work.

As part of her apprenticeship, I had the opportunity to sit down with Laura and talk to her further about her future plans. In our conversation, I pressed her about whether she truly wanted to treat patients. "Do you actually want to check people's ears and throats? Do you want to talk to them about their eating habits and their blood pressure? Do you have a feeling that is really what you want to do with your time and skills?" I encouraged her to be honest with herself. "Don't think about the patients you've seen your dad treat. Now is the time to be real with yourself."

Even though her father and mother supported her goals and did not pressure her, I knew how the subconscious desires to please parents can inform decision-making. I repeated, "Do you really feel like you want to be a doctor?" After careful thought, she responded meekly, "No, not really." I said, "Well, that's it. That's your answer."

I explained how she could still be involved in the medical field without being the practitioner, which could save her at least six years of schooling (plus the massive amounts of debt she would accrue in school). I encouraged her to speak to a friend of mine—who is an entrepreneur and owns multiple medical practices—and schedule meetings with other medical professionals and entrepreneurs to gather different perspectives.

I told her to always pause and reevaluate before leaping into her next. As simple as it sounds, I instructed her to develop a pros and cons list for two areas: being a medical practitioner (professional) versus an entrepreneur (nonprofessional) to discover "What's next?" I encouraged her to continue to be honest with herself and get clarity on what drives her.

Laura had an advantage over some of her peers: a freedom mindset. She was skeptical of doing what the majority does and instead considered how she could get where she wanted to go in the quickest way possible. I reminded Laura that the goal was to take the path of least resistance to get what she wanted in life sooner. That's the key: don't take the well-worn path. Choose the path less traveled.

Like many of our Freedom Founders apprentices, Laura had the aptitude to do just about anything she wanted; yet, she made the intentional decision to give herself the freedom of time and choice before embarking on her career. My hope was that during her in-between year, she would consider whether the traditional path of work and wealth—modeled by her parents—was the right path for her.

The simple act of taking time to think before she acted gave Laura the foundation of a freedom-based mindset. Rather than conceding the traditional career path by default, she took the time to make a fully informed, intentional decision about what was right for her and her future as she began constructing a freedom-based life.

For more information on how I advise young people to approach their career and training, see my book *The Apprentice Model: A Young Leader's Guide to an Anti-Traditional Life.*

THE POWER OF ASKING, "WHAT'S MY NEXT?"

Recently I met with a new couple who wanted to join Freedom Founders. Upon speaking with them, I was impressed by their work ethic and entrepreneurial acumen. Both in their fifties, they had worked together in the practice for some time, but once the practice grew, the husband brought in two other dentists to partner with him. They had twin sons in high school and had created a family-centric life for their children.

In many ways, they represent many of our Freedom Founders members. They have strong values and work ethics and have spent years training to enhance their skills and working to cultivate their businesses. They have a strong reason *why* they want to achieve freedom, and it revolves around their desire to have more time with their family.

Like many of the clients I work with, they were closer to freedom than they thought. They were close to a tipping point of their Freedom Number, but they were really seeking permission to take the next step. They had worked hard and done well and needed help to see how close they were.

As I spoke with the husband, he admitted that he enjoyed dentistry, but it wasn't his passion. His passion, it turned out, was mentoring young people. He had been a swimmer in his youth and was now coaching his sons' swim team. Through coaching, he is investing in his proficiency of communication and leadership. I had no doubt that he was a skilled coach, because in our time together, it was clear he had the ability to bring out the best in people.

He also explained that he had a tight group of friends—his five—who meet early each morning to work out together. Since this group is composed of nondentists, and in fact, is filled mostly with entrepreneurs, he is also building a network and investing in his relationships.

As we talked more about what his next might be, I connected his love of mentoring with his unique business model. He's had success with his partnership model and has organically started instructing other colleagues on how they might do the same thing in their own practices. I said, "You know, that's how Freedom Founders started."

I relayed the story of the Christmas letter Kandace sent out years prior that led my colleagues to start asking for advice on selling their practices. He was intrigued and said he'd never thought of combining mentoring and dentistry to teach other professionals how to adopt his business model.

As we talked, we determined he was about three years away from his Freedom Number, but for him, freedom didn't mean selling his practice. He was enjoying what he'd built, and it was working for him. I asked him how he felt about working three days a week. "I can do that! In fact, if I did, I could do dentistry for another decade and love it!" We decided he would start by taking Fridays off. Then he could transition to a three-day workweek for three years. After that, he should have reached freedom and could make whatever choices aligned with his greater purpose.

As far as mentoring, I encouraged him not to wait three years to begin thinking about "What's next?" I said, "Here's the key— don't wait. Start it now. You have two or three buddies who've been reaching out to you. Pick a weekend, invite them out, and talk about what you've done. Let them ask questions. That's going to be your start." From there, I knew he would know "What's next?"

That's how you do it. It's not a secret formula. You don't wait until the time is perfect; you don't wait until you have it all figured out. Those are rare days you may never see. You have to start with what your idea is now.

This dentist's freedom didn't include stepping away from his work, and that's fine. The important thing was that he was being honest with himself about his goals—which for him included continuing to do the thing—not because he had to, but because it contributed to his meaning, purpose, and significance.

His next was mentoring, but he needed permission to do so. He also needed to realize that his next didn't mean leaving dentistry or selling his practice but moving to a three-day-per-week partnership that allowed him a relaxed schedule, while exploring his mentoring platform. We agreed he would pilot test a mentoring program now because if he waited three years before making this move, he wouldn't be ready. By starting now, he's generating positive feedback that will undoubtedly drive him to his next sooner rather than later.

This couple modeled how you start today building your freedom for tomorrow. You get honest with yourself, get your vision clarified, and create specific goals. As this couple learned, so much of a freedom mindset is about giving yourself permission to be different and then removing the barriers, real or not, that are preventing you from moving forward to your next.

> So much of a freedom mindset is about giving yourself permission to be different and then removing the barriers, real or not, that are preventing you from moving forward to your next.

It's the financial piece that typically holds people back from moving faster to their next. They procrastinate, they hold back, they wait until everything is "right" before even considering taking action.

You have to first be honest with yourself and not live by others' expectations. You want to move toward the top of the Five Freedoms—financial, time, relationships, health, and purpose. The time to act is now. So get started.

THE ANTITRADITIONAL LIFE

Freedom is doing what you want to do, when you want to do it, and with whom you want to do it. Sounds great, doesn't it? Does it happen automatically? No. Is it something we're taught in school? Absolutely not.

A good indicator of how trapped you are by your career is how you feel on Sunday evening. Are you stressed, anxious, and full of dread about the workweek? If so, you're not living a life true to yourself; you're just doing a job. As we've discussed, we all have a sacrifice period when we trade time for dollars. The problem is getting trapped there. As Henry David Thoreau says, that mindset leads to "lives of quiet desperation."[13]

Here's a hard reality: the majority doesn't want you to succeed. They want you to remain with them, living lives of quiet desperation, upholding the status quo. But remember, you get what you accept. If you're willing to accept the path of the majority, then accept the mediocrity that comes with it.

For many years, I traveled the road well traveled—meaning, I followed the majority. I followed all the rules. I was a conformist. I trusted what I was told and believed it to be the truth. And that road worked for me—until it didn't.

Why play bigger? Why make myself uncomfortable if I don't have to? Shouldn't I have permission to coast at some point? Sure, but it's a choice. I've since realized that I can't coast. It's not in my DNA (and probably not in yours either if you're reading this).

It's not easy to go against the grain. It's not easy to walk away from good people with wrong mindsets. It's not easy to stray from the safety of the majority. But if you're ever going to break the chains, you

---

13 Henry David Thoreau, *Walden* (New York: SDE Classics, 2018), 4.

have to commit to showing up, and more often than not, showing up as a different you—stepping beyond your own norm. Easy? Hell no! Life altering? Absolutely!

When you live according to other people's agendas, you waste your life, and as I learned during my daughter's illness, time is the greatest reward. This is why the goal is to reach a Freedom Lifestyle sooner, not later, in life. To do that, you need to upend the old model of working a decades-long career you may not like to *somehow, someday* live the life you desire.

Rather than sacrificing your entire life, the "What's next?" approach turns the traditional model on its head and challenges "Why not?" Why not build a Freedom Lifestyle that benefits yourself, your relationships, and your legacy and allows time for exploration and meaning?

When you have ideas that others label "antitraditional," embrace them. If people tell you something cannot be done or shouldn't be done, don't accept that as an absolute answer. Those will merely create more obstacles for you to overcome on your quest for freedom. The best advice I can give? Trust, but verify. Question everything. Be discerning. Never settle.

My mentor, Dan Kennedy, says, "Most people get stopped too easily. Most people give up on their dreams without putting up much of a fight."[14] Give yourself permission to choose a different path and to think differently. If someone questions your path, put up a fight, as Kennedy encourages, so that you don't impede your own potential. Isn't your time, family, and purpose worth fighting for?

Freedom Founders is a counterculture that challenges the traditional path to wealth building, the self-limiting mindset, and

---

14   Dan S. Kennedy, *My Unfinished Business* (Charleston: Advantage Media Group, 2009), 230.

the widespread indoctrination of our educational and professional trainings models. I want to change the way people think about their lives and their freedom, not just for professionals but for all people.

IN FREEDOM FOUNDERS, WE BELIEVE

- that your greatest risk is doing nothing at all;
- time is the most precious asset;
- in owning the course of your life;
- you can complete your freedom plan in three to five years;
- financial friends are your best insurance policy;
- you become the average of the five people with whom you most associate;
- in a strong sense of community;
- now is the best time to start;
- in doing the right thing, not the easy thing;
- a board of advisers is better than a guru *all day long*;
- gratitude is the beginning of freedom;
- life's better when you aren't a slave to your business;
- strong relationships are the foundation for personal freedom;
- you'll never regret spending more time with family;
- you can't change a person's performance until you change their beliefs;
- in less information and more implementation;
- your network is your net worth;

- the majority is usually wrong;

- fear is the enemy of freedom;

- passive income is better than active income; and

- it's not too late—you're closer than you think.

There's a bigger, more exciting life out there for anyone who adopts the "What's next?" mindset. Once you can free yourself from a scarcity mindset, all the good things in life expand. Your world and your network expand too because you're not stuck in a career trap. You have time and relationship freedom. You have the energy and excitement to make a bigger influence.

I thank you for taking the time to learn more about the Freedom Founders Blueprint for an antitraditional lifestyle. In over forty years of blazing a trail through the alternative investing wilderness (eternally guided by the shining light of freedom) and helping hundreds of dentists and professionals follow the path to achieve their own freedom, I've discovered those who reach their freedom goals the fastest all shared one trait in common: they took massive action. The moment they saw a path through, they charged forward, not always knowing what was around the bend. But what they discovered around the bend changed their lives. It can change yours too.

> I've discovered those who reach their freedom goals the fastest all shared one trait in common: they took massive action.

Dan Kennedy says, "If you would like to know what I've decided is the single biggest difference between successful people and 'the mediocre majority,' between leaders and followers, between those who enjoy generally rewarding lives versus those who lead mostly frustrating lives, here it is: how easily they take 'no' for an answer. If you wanted to focus on the one single behavior that has more to do with success than any other, this is it."[15]

Don't settle for what "the mediocre majority" offers you, unless you've resigned yourself to an average life. Don't wait for *someday*. There's no such day in the week. You have to start today. The place to start is where you are. Time waits for no one, so start now. Your freedom is waiting.

---

15   Dan S. Kennedy, *My Unfinished Business* (Charleston: Advantage Media Group, 2009), 234

RESOURCES

Suggested readings:

- *Change or Die* by Alan Deutschman
- *The E Myth: Why Most Businesses Don't Work and What to Do about It* by Michael Gerber
- *Think and Grow Rich* by Napoleon Hill
- *The Super General Dental Practice* by Dr. Mike Abernathy
- *The Profit Book* by Davy Tyburski
- *Profit First* by Michael Michalowicz
- *The Bezos Letters* by Steve Anderson
- *EntreLeadership* by Dave Ramsey
- *No B.S. Ruthless Management of People and Profits* by Dan Kennedy
- *No B.S. Direct Marketing* by Dan Kennedy
- *Start with Why* by Simon Sinek
- *Turn the Ship Around* by David Marquet

- *From Good to Great* by Jim Collins
- *Extreme Ownership* by Jocko Willink and Leif Babin
- *Simple Numbers* by Greg Crabtree
- *Scaling Up* by Verne Harnish
- *Traction* by Gino Wickman
- *The One Thing* by Gary Keller
- *Focus* by Al Ries
- *Zero to One* by Peter Thiel
- *The Power of Authority* by Michele Prince
- *Go Slow to Grow Fast* by Brent R. Tilson
- *Finish Big* by Bo Burlingham
- *Built to Sell* by John Warrilow
- *Building a Story Brand* by Donald Miller
- *The Heart of a Leader* by Ken Blanchard
- *The Liberty of Our Language Revealed* by Thomas Blackwell
- *Flip the Script* by Oren Klaff
- *Unstoppable* by Chris Zook
- *The Lean Start Up* by Eric Ries
- *Can't Hurt Me* by David Goggins
- *Halftime* by Bob Buford
- *The Culture of Success* by Steven J. Anderson
- *The Five Dysfunctions of a Team* by Patrick Lencioni
- *Rich Dad Poor Dad* by Robert Kiyosaki

- *Real Estate Investing Gone Bad* by Phil Pustejovsky

- *Linchpin* by Seth Godin

- *Looking Forward to Monday* by Adam Witty

- *Almost Alchemy* by Dan Kennedy

- *From High Income to High Net Worth for Dentists: The Ultimate Guide to Gain Freedom in Your Life with More Time Off, Less Stress, Security & Peace of Mind* by Dr. David Phelps

- *The Apprentice Model: A Young Leader's Guide to an Anti-Traditional Life* by Dr. David Phelps

- *Selling Your Practice* by Dr. David Phelps

OUR SERVICES

Whenever you're ready, here are some other ways I can help fast-track you to your freedom goal (you're closer than you think):

1. **Hear more from me through books, podcasts, and blogs**

   □ *From High Income to High Net Worth for Dentists: The Ultimate Guide to Gain Freedom in Your Life with More Time Off, Less Stress, Security & Peace of Mind* by Dr. David Phelps, HighIncomeBook.com

   □ *The Apprentice Model: A Young Leader's Guide to an Anti-Traditional Life* by Dr. David Phelps, ApprenticeModelBook.com

   □ *The Dentist Freedom Blueprint* podcast, DentistFreedomBlueprint.com

   □ Quick-hitting videos and articles for those looking to jump-start their freedom journey. Visit FreedomFounders.com/Blog.

2. Schedule a call with me

If you'd like to replace your active practice income with passive investment income within two to three years, and you have at least $1 million in available capital (can include residential / practice equity or practice sale), then go the following link to schedule a quick call with my team. If it looks like there is a mutual fit, you'll have the opportunity to schedule a call with me directly: FreedomFounders.com/Schedule.

3. Get your free Retirement Scorecard

Benchmark your retirement and wealth building against hundreds of other practice professionals and get personalized feedback on your biggest opportunities and leverage points. Go to FreedomFounders.com/Scorecard to take the three-minute assessment and get your scorecard.

4. Apply to visit the Freedom Founders Mastermind Group

If you'd like to join dozens of dentists, doctors, and practice professionals on the fast track to freedom (three to five years or less), visit FreedomFounders.com/Step-1 to apply for a guest seat.

5. Work with me directly

If you'd like to work directly with me and a small group of my closest investment colleagues, with direct access to the dealmakers and asset classes that I invest in, just send a message to admin@freedomfounders.com and put "Fast Access" in the subject line. Or call (972) 203-6960 (ext. 160) and leave a brief voice mail. Let us know you're interested in the Fast Access program—we'll set up a time with you to talk, find out about your goals, and see if there is a fit.

6. Receive a case study package.

SPECIAL OPPORTUNITY

GET YOUR INFORMATION PACKET WITH
CASE STUDIES OF REAL PRACTITIONERS
BUILDING WEALTH OUTSIDE WALL STREET

 YES! I WANT TO RECEIVE A FREE INFORMATION PACKAGE WITH CASE STUDIES OF DENTISTS AND ORTHODONTISTS WHO ARE REPLACING ACTIVE INCOME FROM THEIR PRACTICE WITH TRUE INVESTMENT CASH FLOW THAT ISN'T TIED TO THE WALL STREET ROLLER COASTER.

THIS CASE STUDY PACKAGE WILL SHOW YOU ...

- HOW PRACTITIONERS ARE BUILDING WEALTH AND CASH FLOW,

- WHAT IT LOOKS LIKE TO CONTROL HASSLE-FREE REAL ESTATE WITHOUT THE OWNERSHIP HEADACHES,

- WHY THE "TRADITIONAL" RETIREMENT MODEL IS FAILING PRACTITIONERS, AND HOW TO ADAPT TO A POST-WALL STREET INVESTING ERA, AND

- A NEW PATH TO INVESTING OUTSIDE OF WALL STREET.

TELL US WHERE TO SHIP IT, AND WE'LL GET YOUR PACKAGE IN THE MAIL RIGHT AWAY!

- CLAIM ONLINE AT: FREEDOMFOUNDERS.COM/CASESTUDY

- CLAIM BY CALL OR TEXT AT: (972) 203-6960 (EXT. 141)

- CLAIM BY FAXING THIS FORM TO: (972) 771-5508

- CLAIM BY EMAIL: ADMIN@FREEDOMFOUNDERS.COM
  (PUT "CASE STUDY REPORT" IN THE SUBJECT LINE)

SEND MY FREE CASE STUDY REPORT TO:

NAME _____

BILLING ADDRESS _____

CITY _____ STATE _____ ZIP _____

PHONE _____ EMAIL _____

7. **Visit us online**

You can find more resources like these at FindYourNext. com/Resources. Let us help you find your next.

ACKNOWLEDGMENTS

For this particular "next" in my life, I'd like to extend my thanks to the following people:

Dr. John Mark Weaver, "The Chief," who offered to me the following advice in 1979: "If you fail to plan, you plan to fail." Thank you, Chief, for being my wingman all these years. The plan is still unfolding. You are most appreciated. "Ride on!"

John Groom, CPA, who saw something of value in me at a very young age when I knew nothing but had big aspirations of doing something more than the majority or status quo. "Stop thinking like a dentist!"

John Schaub, Peter Fortunato, and Jimmy Napier—part of the Florida Six-Pack—who, along with Jack Miller, developed my mindset and financial acumen at a very young age and taught me that I could create my own financial future.

Glenn Stromberg and Ryan Parson, two longtime real estate colleagues who had enough faith to join me when Freedom Founders was only a small speck of an idea.

Robert Brace, Alex Lerma, Nathan Webster, Davy Tyburski,

Lindsey Cope, and Chris Scappatura, who believed enough in me and the Freedom Founders mission to join the ranks to build the Freedom Founders community, even when, at times, it seemed a faraway dream.

Dr. Michael Abernathy, a colleague, friend, and mentor, who provided significant guidance to me in reinventing my failed practice sale and who has been a supporter for the Freedom Founders' movement from day one.

Mike Zlotnik, "Big Mike," with whom I became fast friends at our first Collective Genius meeting and who has remained a steady and faithful supporter and mentor.

Mike Crow, Carrie Wilkerson, James Malinchak, Jonathan Sprinkles, David Frey, Jason Medley, Cory Boatright, Jim Ingersoll, Jim Palmer, Scott Corbett, Eddie Speed, Walter Wofford, H. Quincy Long, Rich Schefren, Dyches Boddiford, Jonathan "Coach JC" Conneely, and Bryan Binkholder, each of whom provided significant inspiration, coaching, and direction in gaining clarity to determine my "next."

My Freedom Founders members, past and present, who continue to believe in me and our mission and provide the clarity as to why I do what I do. You are my people. I love every one of you for who you are and for your commitment to freedom and legacy.

Dr. John Harasin and his beautiful and supporting wife, Jeannie, who were early adopters of our mission and who became leaders in the group as well as our first Free for Life members. Your belief and perseverance in our ideals will continue to serve others and be your mission going forward. Godspeed to you!

My many real estate colleagues and Freedom Founders' Trusted Advisors, who bring integrity, experience, and a service-first approach to our members. Your network is your net worth!

The Advantage|ForbesBook team of Adam Witty, Elaine Best, Laura Rashley, and my cowriter, Summer Flynn. You made the process of taking my passion and vision to a readable text, a project that was a pleasure. When are we doing the next one? ☺

ABOUT THE AUTHOR

David Phelps, DDS, owned and managed a private dental office for over twenty-one years. While still in dental school, he began his investment in real estate by joint venturing with his father on their first rental property in 1980. Three years later, they sold the property, and David took his $25,000 capital gain profit share and leveraged it into thirty-one properties over fifteen years that produced over $15,000 net passive cash flow per month.

After multiple health crises suffered by his daughter, Jenna (leukemia, epilepsy, and a liver transplant at age twelve), David decided to leave his practice so that he could spend time with her. Unfortunately, a divorce and a failed practice sale provided additional setbacks that he had to think and work through.

Today, David is a nationally recognized speaker on creating freedom, building real businesses, and investing in real estate. He also combines his professional and personal experiences to illustrate how the tactical and aspirational work together. David helps other logical, rational professionals become dreamers, then strategically manifest those dreams into freedom. He authors a monthly newsletter, *Path to Freedom*, and hosts the *Dentist Freedom Blueprint* podcast. The Freedom Founders Mastermind community grows year over year, providing the pathway to freedom for many professional practice owners and small business owners.

MORE FROM DR. DAVID PHELPS:

David's website:
DoctorPhelps.com

David's monthly newsletter:
PathToFreedomNewsletter.com

David's weekly podcast:
DentistFreedomBlueprint.com

David's weekly blog:
FreedomFounders.com/Blog

David's Facebook page:
Facebook.com/DrDPhelps

David's YouTube channel:
YouTube.com/User/DrDPhelps